MW01073511

"*Madame Pamita's Magical Tarot*, with its mix of solid knowledge including comprehensive listings of symbols and positive energetic framework, gives a modern twist to the early handbooks of tarot reading, including the work of the legendary Eden Gray."

—Rachel Pollack, author of
The Fissure King: A Novel in Five Stories

"Madame Pamita has a style and voice that bring fun and power to the tarot. Her unique insights take your relationship with the tarot to a new magical level. I can't wait to bring more of her teaching into my own magical practice."

—Jacki Smith, founder of Coventry Creations,
creator of the Blessed Herbal Candles, and author
of *Coventry Magic with Candles, Oils, and Herbs*

"You may have read other books on tarot, but this one is different. It focuses on a positive interpretation of all the cards and shows how to use that energy to transform your life. Whether it's opening up to universal guidance or giving you important lessons for your soul's growth, this book offers a practical road map to personal spiritual evolution."

—Ainslie MacLeod, author of
The Instruction: Living the Life Your Soul Intended

"This is a field guide to otherworldly lands. Your travels are guaranteed to enrich even the most mundane of everyday experiences. All you need are *Madame Pamita's Magical Tarot* and a tarot deck to enter on this grand adventure to a world peopled by wise guides and mystical beings."

—Mary K. Greer, author of *21 Ways to Read a Tarot Card*

"After two decades of studying the tarot, I finally have in my hands a complete manual that brings together all parts of the tarot as one—both theory (its spirit) and practice (its body), as well as its divinatory use and its little-known use in the magical arts. In her book *Madame Pamita's Magical Tarot*, Madame Pamita comfortably walks the deepest labyrinths of magical occultism and deciphers, card by card, the hidden metaphysics of the deck including the most confusing and, in some cases, forgotten ones. She explains all with a coherent ease that is extremely accessible to all seekers of knowledge.

"When you have spent so many years studying and practicing the tarot or any other divinatory science, it can be beneficial to do a refreshing 're-study' of it and explore different points of view. You will find hundreds of manuals teaching how to read the tarot, most of them very good, but with *Madame Pamita's Magical Tarot*, you finally have the opportunity to learn directly from someone who sees the tarot, not only as an oracle, but as a living tool or even as a key to access the entire wisdom of the cosmos, charged with its own spirit and personality. In these pages, wise Madame Pamita will help you discover a complex series of practices that you may have previously ignored and that will make your life much easier in numerous ways. Once you read this book, you will not see your tarot deck the same way. It will evolve from its role as an answering oracle to becoming an extension of yourself and an important part of your day-to-day life."

—Elhoim Leafar, author of
The Magical Art of Crafting Charm Bags:
100 Mystical Formulas for Success,
Love, Wealth, and Wellbeing

Madame Pamita's Magical Tarot

MADAME PAMITA'S
Magical Tarot

Using the Cards
to Make Your Dreams
Come True

MADAME PAMITA

WEISER
BOOKS

This edition first published in 2018 by Weiser Books, an imprint of
Red Wheel/Weiser, LLC
With offices at:
65 Parker Street, Suite 7
Newburyport, MA 01950
www.redwheelweiser.com

Copyright © 2018 by Madame Pamita
All rights reserved. No part of this publication may be reproduced
or transmitted in any form or by any means, electronic or mechanical,
including photocopying, recording, or by any information
storage and retrieval system, without permission in writing from
Red Wheel/Weiser, LLC. Reviewers may quote brief passages.

ISBN: 978-1-57863-629-7
Library of Congress Cataloging-in-Publication Data available upon request.

Cover design by Jim Warner
Cover photograph © Wayne Pierce
Tarot card images derived from the Waite Deck created by Red Wheel/Weiser, LLC
Interior by Steve Amarillo / Urban Design LLC
Typeset in Adobe Sabon, Emigre Dalliance, FF DIN Pro

Printed in Canada
MAR
10 9 8 7 6 5 4 3 2 1

To Morgan and Miles
who make my life magical
every day.

Contents

Acknowledgments

Like sailing a ship, writing a book takes a whole crew. I like to think of my ship as being a magical schooner filled with a crew of happy lady pirates (with a guy or two around to keep things interesting!).

An unending flow of gratitude and appreciation to the experienced navigator of our brave sailing vessel: my editor, Judika Illes, who has steered the treacherous waters of book creation many, many times as a writer and an editor. With her loving support and encouragement, I knew this maiden voyage would be a success. I also want to thank the rest of the able crew at Weiser Books: Sam McKora, for keeping the shuffleboard game going; Jane Hagaman, for ensuring our treasure map was accurate; and Greg Brandenburgh, for keeping me honest when it comes to the Pirate Code of Conduct.

I also have to thank my First Mate, Judy Pokonosky, who told me in early 2016, "You should write a book," let me laugh at her outrageous idea, and didn't say "I told you so!" after I did write one.

Magical blessings to the keeper of the skeleton keys to the pirate chest, Laura Faeth, who long, long ago told me, "You're a reader," when I didn't even know it myself.

I want to send bushels of gratitude to my amazing clients. Each and every one of you is the real treasure of my life's adventure.

And lastly, a thank you kiss to my mama up in the stars, who bought me my first tarot deck and always let me be the rapscallion I am.

Introduction

When we were children, we dreamed of traveling to magical places where we could go on adventures. We imagined owning mystical items that could bestow special powers and meeting fantasy beings who could grant wishes or give us secret knowledge. As we got older, we put aside those beliefs for more rational thinking: "Reality is what it is, and we just have to muck our way through it as best we can." But, the truth is, magic is real and can transform situations, give us special powers, and impart deep wisdom. Magic is everywhere!

As we grow up, many of us forget how to access this magic and connect to the spirit world. However, some of us remember—while others discover the means to access it again through special spiritual tools. Among the most beautiful means of accessing this wisdom is the tarot. Imagine having something so small that you could put it in your pocket, but so powerful that it would allow you to gain profound spiritual knowledge and manifest a life of happiness, fulfillment, health, and plenty. Think of it as owning a portable gateway to the realm of spirit, a guide to answer our questions, and a map to help us move forward on our soul journey. The tarot is all of these things.

Much more than a device to see the future, the tarot is a powerful book of esoteric knowledge in the form of cards. Unlike most books that lead you through a series of ideas step by step, the tarot is random access. Cards are shuffled, different cards are selected, and when they are laid out, they reveal a new story each time. I have owned tarot decks since I was a little ten-year-old, and even after studying, teaching, and reading them for a living on a daily basis, I have never gotten bored with the cards and what they show me. Like the realm of spirit, the tarot is limitless. It is constantly shifting and revealing new information, new insights, and new opportunities for accessing magic in the world and creating our best experience in this lifetime.

We live in a benevolent Universe, one that wants us to be happy, wants us to experience the highest vibration of love, and knows that we can express ourselves as the light beings that we are. As a teacher of the tarot, I always wanted to find a book to recommend to my students that came from this place of high vibration. One that would not only guide them as to the meanings of the cards from the truly positive perspective that the cards contain, but also show them how they can expand far beyond traditional readings and use the cards as tools for manifesting and attracting the best life experiences ever. I wanted a book for students to take home that would help them absorb the information more deeply than there was time for in class. Even more, I wanted a book that could help others who couldn't take a class with me in person. While there are many useful tarot books out there, the one that I was envisioning didn't exist. However, I know it to be true that if you set clear and light-infused intentions on something, it *will* manifest. Now that book *does* exist—it is the one you are holding in your hands.

My wish for you, dear spiritual explorer, is that this book becomes a beautiful tool that will open up your life in positive and magical ways. That through befriending the tarot and creating deep and meaningful connections with each of the cards, you will gain access to higher spiritual realms and acquire deep inner knowing. That you will remember magic is everywhere and that it is your birthright to be an empowered magician, guided on your soul's perfect path with a powerful tool at your disposal: the magical, mystical, manifesting tarot.

[1]

What Is the Tarot (And How Can It Magically Change Your Life for the Better?)

Have you ever wanted to have a genie in a lamp that you could summon anytime you wanted to make a wish? How about a genie who didn't just grant you three wishes, but unlimited wishes? This genie exists. Maybe not in the Disney movie sense, but there is a source of genie-like magic that exists inside of us and in the Universe around us. Believe it or not, we have the power to have, do, or be anything.

There is a concept that is commonly called "The Law of Attraction," which states that "like attracts like" and our thoughts and beliefs will attract the thing we focus on. So, for example, if you're focused on prosperity and feeling the contented, stable feelings that come with being prosperous, prosperity will come to you. If you're focused on lack, feeling afraid of the future, and worried that you won't have enough, then you are blocking prosperity from coming to you.

Magic is the ritual that focuses your attention on the things that you want to influence. When you light a candle for love, for example, you are focusing your intention on the outcome of having love in your life, using the energetic support of the herbs and oils that you apply to the candle, and even using the color of the candle to support your wish or intention.

Thought and magic can and should be followed up with real world action to get the outcome you are wishing for. It's no use doing a spell for a new job if you're not also sending out applications or resumes. So your magic genie is actually three things that are entirely within your control: positive intention + ritual + action = wishes coming true.

So what does tarot have to do with all of this? If you want to hike to the top of the mountain, it's helpful to have a map showing you which trails are easiest, where the bears live, and how long you might expect to be hiking, so you can bring enough trail mix. Tarot is the map that shows you what steps to take, what to avoid, and what changes are necessary to manifest all those good things you want.

Sometimes in my practice, I have clients who come to me with their dilemmas. For example, they may be wondering how they are going to change careers. When we lay out the cards, we can see where they should be positively focusing their intention, what action they should take to support this aim, and even what ritual would be most helpful for supporting their objective. Tarot is the key to making your wish come true.

The tarot is an ingenious tool. The basics of the system are that you have seventy-eight cards, each with a different meaning and vibration, covering all aspects of our human and spiritual experience. When you shuffle these cards, you intuitively place them in a particular order that will tell a story. You might believe that shuffling is random, but as you delve further into the world of mysticism, you will come to know that there are no coincidences; that the purportedly random incidents of our life actually have profound meaning.

The Swiss psychiatrist, Carl Jung, called these "meaningful coincidences" synchronicities. Synchronicities happen to us all the time just moving through our lives but most of us don't notice them or else we chalk them up as flukes. For example, you may have gotten two job offers—one from the Gap located on Main Street and the other from Sephora located on 5th Avenue. As you're walking down the street, you are thinking about this choice, unsure which one would be best for you. As you are musing on this question, a person stops to ask for directions to Main Street and he's wearing a t-shirt that says "Mind the Gap." Is it a coincidence? Jung and I would say, "No." You were wondering and, in essence, asking the Universe for an answer and a clear answer appeared. You can dismiss it as coincidence, but why not take the Universe up on this magical message?

The tarot is a little more direct than just bumping around out in the world and paying attention to the little things that match up to give us messages. We intentionally sit down and ask a specific question and then shuffle the deck to intuitively order those symbolic and synchronous cards that will give us the answer.

The cards have infinite depth to tell us a story. Each card has a meaning and we interpret and attach that meaning to our question. So, if we have a simple question, we might pull just one card and find our answer in the interpretation of that card. But if we have a more complex question or want to look at our question from multiple angles, then we pull more cards and place them in what is called a *spread* or a *layout*.

A spread is simply cards placed on the table in a certain pattern with each placement having a meaning in addition to the card meaning. For example, you can do a simple three-card spread with the card on the left indicating the influences of the past; the card in the middle, the present; and the card on the right, the future.

Past/Present/Future: A Three-Card Reading

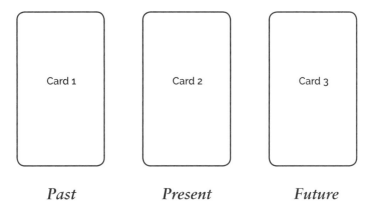

| Card 1 | Card 2 | Card 3 |

Past   *Present*   *Future*

We can go to amazing depths in a reading and in the specific kinds of messages that we get. We start that recipe with the question, we then add the meaning of each of the cards that we turn up, next we add another layer of meaning with the position of the cards in the layout, and then we add the final layer of meaning by listening to what our intuition has to say about the matter.

All of these levels of looking at a reading might sound intimidating now, but we are going to break it all down, and by the time you've finished this exciting adventure, you'll be opening up to understanding the tarot in ways that you never thought possible. With a little openness to going on this wonderful journey, it won't be long before you're getting and giving spiritual and practical guidance for those all-important life questions and accessing amazing intuitive wisdom.

[2]

The Prequel
to Our Adventure

*L*ike most great adventures, there's an important origin story to learn before we jump into the action. And the history goes way back. The oldest documented tarot decks originated in Northern Italy in the early to mid-1400s, originally as a card game to be played, not as a fortune-telling device. However, divination itself goes back to the earliest recorded history and there is evidence of people in Spain telling fortunes using playing cards dating from the same era as the oldest tarot. So, while the tarot may not have been initially intended and designed for intuitive work, it seems quite possible that people may have latched onto it early on as a tool for opening up intuition.

These original tarot decks were like an expanded version of modern playing cards. There were four suits like our spades, clubs, hearts, and diamonds. There were *pip cards* that were numbered Ace through ten. And there was a group of *court cards* similar to our Jack, Queen, and King. There was also an additional group of twenty-two cards that we don't see in our fifty-two card deck called the *trumps*. Each of these trump cards had an archetypal image such as The Sun, The Empress, or the Wheel of Fortune.

To understand how the tarot became the esoteric tool that we know today, you need to know a little about the history of magic and of underground spirituality, otherwise known as the occult. In ancient civilization, spirituality and science were often intertwined. In ancient Egypt and Greece, for example, illness was treated with both medicine and magic. This would later evolve into alchemy, which was something like scientific research with spiritual and magical elements thrown in.

Let's fast-forward into the 1700s in Europe during the Age of Enlightenment. This era saw the birth of science as we know it today, and also began the division between science and spirituality. However, as people became more scientific, certain segments of the population still remained committed to what had evolved into an underground spirituality, and secret societies such as the Freemasons and Rosicrucians blossomed. These secret societies relied heavily on symbolism and ritual and during this era, when the interest in mysticism was so high, we start to see the first published guides to using the tarot for divination.

During the late 1800s, a secret society focused on magic and ancient spiritual secrets was formed called the Golden Dawn. The founders of the Golden Dawn included some Masons and Rosicrucians who emphasized spiritual awakening through the understanding of astrology, alchemy, divination, and, not surprisingly, the tarot.

In the early 1900s, Arthur Edward Waite, a member of the Golden Dawn, decided to publish an innovative new tarot deck. He was inspired by the *Sola Busca*, a deck from the late 1400s that incorporated images on all the cards, not just the trump cards. He commissioned the illustrator, Pamela Colman Smith, who was also a member of the Golden Dawn, to come up with the images for the deck, including designing new ones for the pip cards. These images drew from the symbolic language of the Golden Dawn, Freemasonry, Rosicrucianism, alchemy, and the Jewish mystical tradition known as Kabbalah. The resulting deck was published by Rider and Sons Company and was called the Rider-Waite deck, which may now also be known as the Rider-Waite-Smith or the Waite-Smith deck.

While the Rider-Waite-Smith (RWS) deck is certainly not the only deck available, it is by far the most popular one used today, and is the one I recommend to everyone starting to learn the tarot. It was the first deck that I picked up when I was ten years old, and, even after decades of working with it, the symbolism is so rich that I still discover new meanings in the cards. It's also the deck that most modern decks are based on, so if you learn to read from the RWS, you'll be in an excellent place to read from many other decks. In addition, it's the one that I'll be referring to in this book to help you begin your tarot adventures.

[3]

Your Mystic
Training Begins

For our first adventure with the tarot, we're going on a journey to really get to know the cards. To develop a relationship with a person, you need to have experiences with them and see them in different situations. It's the same with tarot cards. The key is spending time with them. This is truly a "tortoise and the hare" situation where the slow and steady gain deeper knowledge and become better readers than those who rush to the finish line.

I remember when I was just beginning to study the cards, I wanted to rush to the destination of "reader." I didn't want to take the time to be a student. Now that I'm older, I realize the beauty in being that beginner. There is joy in the journey toward gaining knowledge. I look at it as an amazing exploration. I know that going down the road is going to bring me such profound experiences and that eventually, if I take the time to really learn and absorb and apply myself, I can get to the place where I become master of that skill. So, take the time to enjoy these exercises as you unfold your knowledge of the cards and build your connection to them.

There is a question that inevitably comes up when people are learning to read: Should I look up the meaning of the cards or just trust my own intuition? I believe that the best readers incorporate both into their practice.

When I was a little girl, I spent the first few years around the cards just looking at them, talking to them, and playing with them. Then, when I was in my teens, I started studying from books and trying to memorize someone else's definition of the cards. The result was that I became more and more confused as to the meaning of the cards and became paralyzed trying to remember exactly what someone else said the card meant and how that related to the question we were asking in a reading.

Here's a little secret: There is no tarot "Bible" that has the one definitive answer regarding what a particular card means. If you look at ten different books on the cards, they'll give you ten different variations on the definition, which is great, I believe. The cards are open to interpretation, as is the Bible, by the way.

This kind of dynamic, interactive quality is perfect for an intuitive tool. It should be open-ended enough that your own truth can shine through. Book definitions, including the ones in this book, should be viewed as an additional viewpoint to add to your own. When I finally figured this out, I started using books in a very different way.

Think of it like this: Imagine you have a friend at work named Tanya. You know her as a really efficient worker, someone who cracks funny jokes, and who is fun to eat lunch with. Then, you meet someone who knows Tanya outside of work and they tell you she's an amazing dancer—and you love dancing, too. That piece of information adds some richness to your understanding of your work friend, but it doesn't define who she is for you or what your relationship is. It's the same with the cards. Build your own understanding of the cards and let the books add to your relationship instead of defining it.

The first thing that I recommend to help you build this relationship is to keep a daily tarot reading journal. If you focus deeply on one card a day, you will develop a deep and intimate connection to the cards. To begin this exercise, you need a dedicated journal to write in each day. It doesn't matter if the journal is a dollar store spiral notebook or an imported leather-bound book. Use what feels right to you. Every morning, pull one card and write about it in your journal.

1. First, identify whether your card is Major Arcana or Minor Arcana. Don't know which is which? Familiarize yourself with the chapters in this book on the Major Arcana and the Minor Arcana.

2. Write the name of the card at the top of the page.

3. Next, look closely at your card and write down your observations on any or all of the following:

    a. What colors do you see? What emotions do these colors evoke for you?

    b. What people, animals, and objects do you observe in the card? Remember to look beyond the main characters and into the details.

    c. What are the people depicted in the cards wearing? Is there anything unusual in their clothing or accessories?

    d. What symbols do you see? What could these symbols mean?

    e. Does the scene take place indoors or outdoors? What do you see in the environment?

    f. If you stepped into the scene in the card, what would happen? How would you interact with others in the card?

    g. Put yourself in the role of one of the characters in the card. How do you feel?

4. Now, looking at the observations that you've written down, what do you think the card could mean?

5. After you've written down your own interpretation, look up the meaning of the card either in this book or any other books on the tarot. Which definitions click for you? Which ones feel like they make sense, or give you an "Aha!" moment? Listen to your inner guidance and choose the ones that feel good and skip any that don't make sense to you. Once you've determined which ones speak to you, write down those additional key words or phrases that add to your understanding of the card.

6. Now write how you think the energy of this card could possibly show up in your life today.

7. Once you've done the above, close your journal and set it aside.

8. At the end of your day, open the journal again, reflect on how the energy of the card actually showed up in your day, and write a few lines about it. Under the definition for each of the

cards in this book, you'll find "Behind the Mysterious Door—Journal Questions to Explore [the card] More Deeply." After you have written your own initial insights, you may want to reflect in a deeper and more meditative way on the meaning of the card. These journal questions will help you develop a personal relationship to the cards that will enrich your readings tremendously.

By doing a daily practice of looking closely, creating a personal interpretation, adding the knowledge of others, and then relating it to the circumstances of your life, you will be well on your way to becoming an accomplished reader.

[4]

Magic Words

O ne of the most powerful spiritual disciplines that you can incorporate into your life is the practice of saying affirmations. Affirmations are positive power words that we can say to ourselves to rewire our brains, making us magical receptors for good things. This isn't something new. Our word "spell" comes from the Proto-Germanic word *spellan*, which means *to tell*. Spells are words. Words create magic. Magic is the act of shifting reality through our will. Therefore, magic spells are words that create our reality.

Words can shift thoughts and beliefs in the direction that we intentionally want them to flow, and that flow allows good things to come to us.

Your thoughts create your beliefs and your beliefs are infinitely powerful. Imagine someone who thinks that they can't get into college, who believes that they'll never get a degree. Now, what is the likelihood that they graduate with a bachelor's degree? The chances are virtually nil. Because their negative thought was repeated over and over again until it became a belief, it's very unlikely that they would even apply to college, let alone see it through to graduation. As a result, the belief ultimately created the reality.

The same applies to all of us, from the smallest things to the biggest. The thought is the seed of the result. So, one of the best things that we can do for ourselves is to plant the seeds of the results that we wish to see. That's where affirmations come in. We can use affirmations to disrupt negative thought patterns and rewire our brain to create positive beliefs that then bring amazing outcomes.

The basics for working with tarot affirmations are simple and you'll find powerful affirmations for each of the tarot cards right in this book. Beneath the definition for each card, you'll find "Magic Words," a suggested affirmation associated with the energy of that card.

One of the ways that you can begin working with these affirmations is to choose a card at random. Find the affirmation listed under the definition of the card, then look at the card and speak the affirmation out loud to yourself several times. Saying it over and over again increases the new neuron connections that you create in your brain.

But that's like a scoop of vanilla ice cream. There are so many ways you can add sprinkles, nuts, cherries, and sauces to your affirmation. Add on some of these extras to supercharge your affirmation, give it power to manifest extra quickly, and just plain have more fun with it.

Tarot affirmation options:

- Instead of choosing a card at random, choose one based on something you wish to manifest.

- Instead of repeating the affirmation listed in this book, make up your own.

- Speak the affirmation out loud while looking at yourself in the mirror.

- Make copies of the card and place them where you'll see them throughout the day. When you see one, let it be a reminder to repeat the affirmation several times out loud.

- Set an alarm on your phone with the affirmation as the note on the alarm to remind yourself to repeat it throughout the day.

- Take a photo of the card with your phone and place it on your phone's background to remind you of your affirmation every time you pick up your phone.

- Get a trusted person to speak the affirmation to you.

- Start a special Tarot Affirmation Journal—write down the name of the card and then write down some affirmations and intentions of what you wish to manifest based on the card.

[5]

Making Magic
with the Tarot

Affirmations alone are powerful but there are ways to build on that power. Remember when I said that magic is the act of bending reality to our will? A really adept magician can manifest with thought alone, but most of us need help. That's where magical tools come in.

A ritual using a magical tool has the power to focus our thoughts. Think of it like a magnifying glass focusing sunlight into a spot hot enough to set paper on fire. By going through the activity of ritual and using tools that support our outcome, we add power to our thoughts.

The tarot is naturally one of those tools. If you have a deck that you use for readings, then I recommend buying a second deck that you use just for magic or making copies of the cards and using those copies for your spells.

Here are some ways that you can use a tarot card in a spell:

Carry the card with you.

Choose a card that reflects what you would like to manifest and carry it in your pocket or purse—or put it in your shoe.

Place it on an altar.

Set up an altar on a small table in your home or workplace. Place a cloth on the table then arrange a candle, a flower in a vase, and shells, stones, or other talismans in a pleasing way. Choose cards that represent your wishes, dreams, and desires and place them on the altar.

Use it to charge and bless another magical item.

Choose a card that represents your intention and place an item that you wish to charge with that energy on top of the card. The item can be anything, but most people choose things that they can carry such as gemstones, jewelry, feathers, money, flowers, or coins.

Use it to bless your food or drink in a special magical way.

Select a card to represent what you want, then place food such as fruit, vegetables, chocolate, candies, or nuts on top of the card to charge and bless them with the energy of the card. Alternatively, you can place a card over the top of a cup or glass filled with water, coffee, tea, alcohol, or hot chocolate to turn it into a magic potion.

Use it as a meditation focal point.

Set the card of your choice where you can focus on it while meditating. Or look closely at the card, then close your eyes and visualize it in your mind's eye.

Leave in a special place.

You can place a card in a hidden place to imbue that spot with the energy of the card. For example, you could put a love card or a card for healing between your mattress and boxspring or place a card for safety under the seat of your car. You can also secretly hide these cards in public places, such as putting a card representing a promotion in your workplace, or leaving a social justice card in a government building. Likewise, you can place a card in a visible place, such as a prosperity card placed on display in a business with the intent of drawing more customers.

Give it to someone.

You can openly give someone a card with an intent such as healing or love, or secretly slip it into their pocket while they leave their coat unattended.

Place on the body.

You can place a card on a chakra or body part for imbuing that particular point with the energy of the card, such as for healing or empowering.

Use it for dream work.

You can use a card for dream work, either to invite helpful dreams or to do the work in dreamtime, by placing it under your pillow before you go to sleep.

Use it as a petition paper.

A petition paper is a paper on which you write your wishes or intentions. They can be elaborate with words or symbols written in a specific way or as simple as just writing the word or phrase of what you want to bring in or eliminate. A petition written on a tarot card can be placed underneath a candle in a holder, carried in your wallet, or used in any of the other ways mentioned above.

[6]

A Map of the Minor Arcana

So now we get to dive into the deck, learning how it's constructed and interpreting what each of the cards mean. We are going to launch with the part of the tarot whose structure is probably most familiar to you—the Minor Arcana. The tarot is divided into two parts: the Major Arcana and the Minor Arcana. Arcana means "esoteric secrets" so the deck is made up of "major secrets" and "minor secrets." The Major Arcana deal with big-picture themes that we encounter, while the Minor Arcana deal more with our day-to-day experiences and what they mean from a spiritual perspective.

Like regular playing cards, the Minor Arcana is made up of four suits—Swords, Wands, Cups, and Pentacles. Each of the suits has ten numerical cards numbered Ace through ten, or pips, and what we call the court cards—the Page, Knight, Queen, and King, which we will get into in the next section. The tarot suits match up to our playing card suits—Swords to spades, Wands to clubs, Cups to hearts, and Pentacles to diamonds. We have an Ace representing the one, as we do in our playing card deck, as well as a King and Queen. The Page and Knight of the tarot have been smooshed together to make the Jack in the playing card deck.

While every tarot reader divides the tarot into the Major Arcana and the Minor Arcana, I like to divide the Minor Arcana up even further and look at the numbered pip cards and the court cards as separate but related groups. Looking first at the pip cards and then at the court cards will help you to understand these groups and the very different energy that they have.

It's also extremely useful to look at the cards in groups of the suits. Think of the suits being a little like a family, with family characteristics showing up in different ways in each member. Each of the suits has a corresponding element in magic. In ancient times, the elements were a way to classify or understand the world around us and even the world within. The ancients would classify things as Air, Fire, Water, or Earth (sometimes with an additional fifth element of Ether or Spirit), and each of these elements had qualities attached to it that could be used for correspondence. Once you get a handle on understanding the four elements, it will open up a whole new world of symbolism for you to explore.

The first thing that you will have to do is be able to identify the pip cards. The Ace will be an easy one as it says "Ace of [the suit]" at the bottom of the card, but pips two through ten have no words on them at all. In some way, it makes them easy to separate from the rest of the deck as the court cards and the Major Arcana of the RWS all have names on them. In another sense, you will have to dive into them a little deeper to unlock their mysteries. In fact, you will have to think like an ancient Roman to unravel their secrets, or at least learn (or remember) how to read Roman numerals. For those of us who get befuddled at those old movie credits and monuments when we see something like MCMXCVIII, the good news is that for the pips, you only have to know the numbers two through ten and for the Major Arcana, which have the names written on the cards, you have the option of learning the numbers up to 21.

With Roman numerals, the basic thing to understand is that I equals 1, V equals 5, and X equals 10. When a smaller number is to the right, it's added; for example, VI is 5 + 1, or 6. A smaller number to the left is subtracted, for example, IV is 5 − 1, or 4.

Here's a handy chart to help you understand how to break it down.

0	Not defined	
1	I	1
2	II	1 + 1
3	III	1 + 1 + 1
4	IV	5 – 1
5	V	5
6	VI	5 + 1
7	VII	5 + 1 + 1
8	VIII	5 + 1 + 1 + 1
9	IX	10 – 1
10	X	10
11	XI	10 + 1
12	XII	10 + 1 + 1
13	XIII	10 + 1 + 1 + 1
14	XIV	10 – 1 + 5
15	XV	10 + 5
16	XVI	10 + 5 + 1
17	XVII	10 + 5 + 1 + 1
18	XVIII	10 + 5 + 1 + 1 + 1
19	XIX	10 – 1 + 10
20	XX	10 + 10
21	XXI	10 + 10 + 1

Knowing the Roman numerals enables you to know the number, but to know the suit of the card, you'll have to look at the card closely. Like a fortune-teller's game of I Spy, Pamela Colman Smith included the correct number of suit objects in each picture. So, for example, the Six of Cups has six cups included in the illustration. This can come in handy. If you want to double check your Roman numeral knowledge, all you have to do is count the swords, wands, cups, or pentacles on the card to know if you got the number right.

To get really confident with reading the cards, a great practice is to separate the pip cards from the rest of the deck and shuffle them, then start flipping through them at random and identify the number and suit of each card. As each comes up, say the name of the card out loud, such as "Ten of Wands," "Three of Cups," and so on. Keep doing this until they become familiar to you and you don't have to struggle by counting the items.

[7]

The Airy-Fairy Swords

Let's look at the Swords cards and the element of air. Think about the qualities of air. It's the lightest of these four substances that we're talking about. Winds can whip around quickly. Opening a door or window to let in a breeze can freshen up a room. Air is breath and the word "inspiration" literally means to breathe in. The element of air and the suit of Swords represent all these qualities. How did Swords end up representing air? Well, you can imagine the sword waving cleanly and precisely through the air as it's being wielded by a skilled fencer. It's sharp; it's fast; it's defined.

Every time you see a card in the suit of Swords, you can start your interpretation of that card just by thinking of the qualities of air. Air can be a gentle, caressing breeze or a powerful and destructive hurricane. Wind can blow the dust away, it can push the sailing ship forward, and it can carry our messages to far-off places. It supports the bird in flight. It also carries the smoke of incense up to the heavens. Air is literally the medium through which sound passes. No air, no sound. Together air and Swords rule over the realm of thought and communication.

In the world of magic and manifesting your desires, thoughts are the beginning. And a powerful one they are. Everything that has ever been created was first a thought. Ponder that for a second. Can you think of even one thing that was made by a human that didn't first start out as an idea? The chair you're sitting in, the walls around you, the book you're reading right now. All were once just someone's thought. The thought is the seed of everything—everything positive and everything negative. That's why it's so important to pay attention to your own thoughts. What kind of seeds are you planting? Are you reinforcing positive beliefs or are you planting your own seeds of doubt? There's a great saying that's attributed to Henry Ford, "Whether you think you can, or you think you can't—you're right." Your thoughts absolutely can alter and even create your reality. So, when we see a Swords card, it's a wake-up call to pay attention to those thoughts.

Swords also represent communication. Think of the air that leaves your mouth when you speak. Whether the communication is verbal, written, or even electronic, all are the domain of Swords. When we learn magic, we learn the power of the spell. A spell is speaking words of intention. And while thoughts can be powerful internal changers, words are powerful external changers. How many friendships or relationships have suffered because of a harsh word or a miscommunication? And think also of the inspiring words of an eloquent speaker leading people to create change. Or the charming words that can draw a loved one closer. When we communicate, our words have power. This is why speaking a positive affirmation aloud to yourself doubles the power of just thinking that positive thought. And why, when we look at Swords cards, we want to look not just at thought, but also written, verbal, and other kinds of communication. So, as we enter into the world of the Swords, don't forget to think about how these cards reflect the realm of thought and communication.

Your Adventure with the Ace of Swords

Ace of Swords

With a craggy, mountainous landscape in the distance, you see a cloud descend from the sky. From this cloud a hand emerges, holding a silvery sword upright in a gesture of authority and victory. At the top of the sword, a golden crown bedecked in red jewels hovers, draped in an olive branch bearing red olives, and a palm frond. At the hilt of the sword fly six flame-like symbols.

Whenever I see this card, I'm reminded of the Lady of the Lake handing over the magical sword Excalibur to King Arthur. Anyone who has read a book of Arthurian legends or seen the film *Excalibur* will know what I'm talking about. In the film, a mysterious hand emerges from the middle of a lake bearing the magical sword, giving it to Arthur, and establishing his right to rule as king. When you see this card, you can imagine this magical sword being handed to you. You are being given something that is going to elevate your stature, an idea that is going to bring you up into a leadership role. You are being shown the clarity of your noble purpose.

The Ace of Swords represents the pure essence of the element of air and all that it includes: ideas, thoughts, inspiration, logic, communication, mental pursuits, intellect. There is a quality of blessing about all of the Aces, and this Ace represents divine gifts in these particular areas: quick minds, witty words, and pinpoint clarity.

All of the Aces represent a universal "Yes" from Spirit. If the question at hand is a yes/no question, an Ace is a definite "Yes." If more than one Ace shows up in a reading, I interpret that as the Universe saying, "Yes!" with an underline under it!

The jeweled crown hovering around the tip of sword reminds me of the old-fashioned game where you have to catch a small hoop on the end of a stick and when you do, you've won! The crown itself, like all crowns in the tarot, is a connection to divine energy, just as your crown chakra connects your human experience to the heavens. The red jewels, and the red olives, represent ruling over the material world.

The olive branch and palm frond are very old religious symbols. The olive branch represents peace; think of the biblical story of the dove bringing Noah the olive branch as a symbol that Yahweh had made peace with humanity, or the olive being the symbol of Athena, the goddess of wisdom and strategic diplomacy. The palm frond represents sacrifice and victory over death. The sword comes between these two concepts and can be interpreted as intellect mediating between peace and sacrifice.

The sword points up, just like an arrow directing you to "look up there!" It's a "double-edged sword;" our thoughts and words can be used to help or to harm. We have a responsibility to use them for the highest good. The mountains off in the distance will be conquered, but that's for another day. Right now, it's time to bask in your success.

Those six little flamey symbols that are raining down around the sword are called *yods* and are points of divine energy. Yod is the first letter of the Tetragrammaton, the four letters that represents the unpronounceable name of the Creator. In Hebrew mysticism, this letter symbolically represents a blessing. Hebrew letters, like runes, have numerical and symbolic values, as well as indicating sounds. There are three yods on each side of the sword, in perfect balance. Like the scales of justice, this balance represents the fairness of impartial and intellectual judgment.

The Keys to the Treasure Chest—
Key Symbols of the Ace of Swords

Cloud—a spiritual message, clarity emerging from fogginess

Crown—connection to the divine, being the divinely chosen one

Distant mountains—future challenges are conquered through intellect

Hand—Spirit handing this over to you, a firm grasp on logic

Olive branch—peace, reconciliation, wisdom

Palm frond—sacrifice, ultimate victory

Six yods—harmony in the presence of the divine, finding balance, fairness

Sword—clarity, intellect, communication

The Wizard's Words of Wisdom— What the Ace of Swords Signifies in a Reading

Clear communication brings great results

The truth comes out

The Universe is giving you a "Yes"

Use your mind to solve the problem

Victory is being handed to you

Behind the Mysterious Door—Journal Questions to Explore the Ace of Swords More Deeply

What subject do I need to view with impartial clarity?
How can I be more rational about this subject?

Magic Words—Affirmation for the Ace of Swords

"I open up to clarity and truth."

Your Adventure with the Two of Swords

Two of Swords

You are at the edge of a still sea on a calm, clear night with a waxing crescent moon in the sky. At the shoreline, a woman sits on a small stone bench. She is wearing a simple white shift and has a white blindfold covering her eyes. Her arms are crossed in front of her chest and in each hand she holds a large sword.

Seeing a blindfolded woman sitting on the beach holding two giant swords is not something you run across in your daily experiences. The woman is sitting upright and emotionally composed, yet she has her arms crossed in front of her chest. Whenever we see arms crossed, we are looking at someone who is feeling closed off, protective, or even defensive. Not only does this woman have her arms crossed over her heart, but she is also holding a giant sword in each hand. I like to think of her as being on guard for any event. Kind of like the sword masters in the movie *Kill Bill*, she isn't going to be taken by surprise. Yet, when we look at the scene around her, where's the threat? The sky is clear, the sea is calm, and there's nobody else around. That blindfold is preventing her from seeing the reality of the peacefulness and safety of the situation. Yes, there may be rocks to navigate around to get to the shore on the other side, but sailing across a still, calm sea is a joy. When this card pops up, you may be looking at someone who is using logic to close off access to her emotions or being overly protective of her heart. It may not be appropriate or even possible to drop those swords of protection immediately, but if she takes off the blindfold and sees the reality of the safety around her, she may be able to slowly bring down her arms and open up her heart.

Sometimes, this card shows up when we are standing at a crossroads, like the X of her arms. When it does, it indicates that using the rational mind, instead of trusting emotions or being influenced by appearances, is the best way to decide which way to go.

The Keys to the Treasure Chest—
Key Symbols of the Two of Swords

Arms crossed in front of chest—protecting the heart, standing at a crossroads, emotionally closed off

Blindfold—shutting out outside sensation, not seeing things as they are, trusting the intellect completely

Distant shore—goals, destinations

Rocks—navigating around snares and snags

Sea—calm emotion, still waters run deep

Stone bench—desiring stability, groundedness, overly rigid

Swords—being of two minds, using intellect over emotion, crossed communication

Waxing crescent moon—increase

Woman in white dress—simplicity, serenity

The Wizard's Words of Wisdom—
What the Two of Swords Signifies in a Reading

It's okay to slowly open your heart

The reality may not be apparent

These decisions require engaging the intellect

Things are not as scary as they may seem

You are protecting your heart

Behind the Mysterious Door—
Journal Questions to Explore the Two of Swords More Deeply

Where am I afraid to open my heart? What safety can I create that will allow me to open up more?

Magic Words—Affirmation for the Two of Swords

"When I look within, I know that my heart is safe and whole."

Your Adventure with the Three of Swords

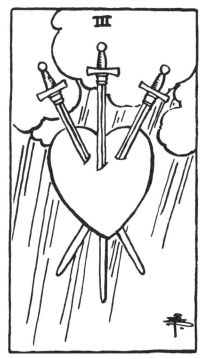

Three of Swords

As we look into the sky, we see gray clouds pouring down rain. In the foreground, we see a large red heart with three swords stuck in it.

This is one of those cards that can give you a visceral feeling. Those three swords poking through the heart almost make us want to clutch our chests and say, "Ouch!" It's not hard to discern that this card can be about emotional pain and heartache. As dramatic as that image is, it's important to look closer at the combination of symbols we see here. First, swords are stabbing the heart—that means that thoughts or communication may have gotten us to this place of pain. The question to ask when this card comes up is, how does my thinking contribute to my pain? If we look more closely at the heart, there's no blood dripping from it, and, other than the swords, it looks like it's in pretty good shape. When this card makes an appearance, we may realize that the beliefs we have about something are the source of the pain—that we are contributing to our own suffering through our thoughts. We can almost imagine pulling out those swords and watching the heart emerge as good as new.

Those rain clouds are significant, too. Stormy weather doesn't last forever, eventually the sun comes out again. And it's good to remember that it's the same thing with pain; things will change and we will eventually feel better.

When this card appears, it's a reminder that our thoughts are the seed of our reality. Sometimes we hold thoughts that create our own suffering, so the Three of Swords reminds us that we have the power to pull out those thoughts like the weeds that they are and plant something that is more hopeful.

The Keys to the Treasure Chest—
Key Symbols of the Three of Swords

Clouds—clouded thinking, things getting in the way, spiritual work

Heart—emotions, feelings, sensitivities, love

Rain—tears, transient pain

Stabbing swords—pain, suffering, negative thoughts or words leading to negative emotion

The Wizard's Words of Wisdom—
What the Three of Swords Signifies in a Reading

Stop beating yourself up

The hurt will pass

You have a choice in how you feel

You have the ability to remove your painful thoughts

Your suffering is unnecessary

Behind the Mysterious Door—Journal Questions
to Explore the Three of Swords More Deeply

Where does my heart hurt? What beliefs do I hold that contribute to this pain?

Magic Words—Affirmation for the Three of Swords

"I easily release painful thoughts and replace them with healing ones."

Your Adventure with the Four of Swords

Four of Swords

You enter into an old medieval church, peaceful, quiet, and still. Inside, you see a sparkling window with a scene of blessing depicted. Below, you see the tomb of a medieval knight. The tomb has a carving of the knight resting in repose, his hands touching in prayer. On the side of the tomb is a carving of a single sword, while above the tomb is a plaque on the wall with a carving of three more swords.

If you have ever been inside an old Gothic cathedral in Europe, you will have a deep understanding of what this card means. When you walk into these old churches, there is a hush that comes over you. Not only is everyone around you quiet and reverent, but there is also an internal sort of quiet that these places exude. It has everything to do with Spirit. You don't have to be a Christian to feel the still, contemplative energy of the spiritual people who have passed through the doors and into this place of prayer. The coolness of the stone walls, the colorful flecks of light that play through the windows, the carved wooden chairs and benches all invite you to sit down and take a look within.

One of the interesting features of these cathedrals is the fact that many of them not only served as places of prayer, but also as places where honored people were buried. As you walk across the stone floor, often you are walking over flat carved stones that say the name and dates for the person who is buried below. People who had the money to spend, would go one step beyond this and commission raised tombs, often with elaborate and idealized renditions of the person residing within. That's what we are seeing on this card—one of those carved stone tombs, showing the image of the knight who is resting in peace inside.

This card isn't indicative of death, however. Its essence is that of peace, rest, and contemplation, the feeling we get when we go into one of those old cathedrals. The swords of thought are still, resting on the wall and on the side of the tomb. When this card shows up for you, it's a reminder to go within, rest, meditate, and most importantly, because this is a Swords card, contemplate.

The act of contemplation that the Four of Swords references is not the same as ruminating with anxious thoughts spinning around in your head. It is the calm reflection of visioning your future into being. The stained-glass window in the background shows a saint blessing a kneeling figure. This beautiful window with the light shining through represents mentally focusing on the blessings that you have in your life right now and also the blessings that you want to envision for your future.

The Keys to the Treasure Chest— Key Symbols of the Four of Swords

Armor—the end of an inner war, a time of peace

Blessing figure in window—blessings that are to come

Body in repose—rest, relaxation, sleep, meditation

Kneeling figure in window—blessings that you have received

Stained-glass window—envisioning your future

Tomb—stillness, quiet, solitude, cocooning

The Wizard's Words of Wisdom— What the Four of Swords Signifies in a Reading

Give your racing thoughts a rest

It's time for thinking, not acting

Rest and recuperate

Slow down

Vision your future into being

Behind the Mysterious Door—Journal Question to Explore the Four of Swords More Deeply

What can I do to bring more serenity into my life?

Magic Words—Affirmation for the Four of Swords

"My stillness is the perfect place to create new dreams."

Your Adventure with the Five of Swords

Five of Swords

You walk along a shoreline under a sky filled with bizarre clouds rising in the distance. You see three men standing on the beach. In the distance, a man with his back to you holds his face in his hands in despair. A bit nearer is another man, also with his back to you, who looks pensively out at the water. Nearest is a man with three swords in his hands, while two more lie at his feet. This man has a smirk on his face as he looks over at the man facing the sea.

This card is filled with delicious ambiguity—first of all, that bizarre sky. Those jagged clouds seem to mirror the tension in the scene below. Their angle makes it look as if the world is off-kilter. Or are they even clouds at all? It's very conceivable that we're looking at smoke coming off multiple fires. If there was a battle, it could be strategic locations that were set ablaze.

With all the swords lying around, it's clear that the three men have been in combat of some sort. Why does the one in the foreground have all the swords? Were they the winners or the losers in the battle? Were they battling with each other or are they fighting on the same side and have just finished battling someone else? Or are the three men actually three versions of the same warrior seen over time and space as he first feels smug at his victory, then deeply contemplates what he has done, then feels sadness and remorse?

Any one of these interpretations can show up in a reading of this card. Needless to say, while there are a lot of different ways this card can be interpreted, none of these scenarios looks like a decisive victory. These three have just finished a battle where some things were lost, represented by the man in despair; and some things were gained, represented by the smirking, self-satisfied sword holder; while the man in the middle-ground questions whether it was all worth it.

Sometimes in our lives, we see this kind of gain and loss that produces no net result. We work hard to make money that goes straight out to pay the bills. We invest time and energy in getting an education but then get a job in a completely different field where our degree makes no difference. We put tons of effort into a relationship, hoping that it will move things forward but it seems to be at a standstill. I call this the "mouse on the wheel" effect. We are running, running, running but seem to be getting nowhere. We are battling something tooth and nail but still not seeing a decisive victory.

When this card appears, it's time to take stock. Where are we investing our time, energy, thoughts, our heart, or our money and what is it producing? If we're like that mouse running on the wheel, this card is a sign that it's time to get off that wheel, change strategies, and try approaching our objectives in a different way. Or it may be a signal to trade the present goal for a new one. It's not about abandoning something, but more about refining your approach. Look at what works and what doesn't and quit spending your time and energy on things that are not bringing you the rewards that you want.

This card can also warn about time stealers and energy vampires. These are activities and people who distract you and take you away from your aims. Watch out for those bright and shiny things that pull you into their tractor beam (social media, anyone?) and resist the temptation to get pulled off your path.

The Keys to the Treasure Chest—
Key Symbols of the Five of Swords

Contemplative man—thinking over the costs of the battle

Distant land—goals and objectives

Man with face in hands—despair

Sea—deep emotion

Smirking man—*schadenfreude*, joy in someone else's misery

Smoke/jagged clouds—obscuring the truth, confusion

Swords—conflicting thoughts

The Wizard's Words of Wisdom—
What the Five of Swords Signifies in a Reading

Assessing whether energy expended is producing results

Avoiding distractions that don't help you reach your goals

Choosing your battles wisely

Experiencing indecisive victories

Facing internal or external conflict

Behind the Mysterious Door—Journal Questions
to Explore the Five of Swords More Deeply

Where am I spinning my wheels? What new strategy
can I implement?

Magic Words—Affirmation for the Five of Swords

"I resolve my problems with new and creative solutions."

Your Adventure with the Six of Swords

Six of Swords

You watch as a ferryman pushes a small flat-bottom boat across a lake with a long pole. Two passengers huddle in the boat in front of him—a small child and an adult wrapped in a cloak. They are surrounded on front and sides by a "fence" made up of six swords. They are in choppy water, but up ahead, the lake is smooth. In the distance, we see a far shore with small groves of trees on it.

This card indicates that, while things are challenging now, with some help or effort you will move into tranquil and uncomplicated circumstances. Are you the ferryman pushing things forward or are you the passengers, receiving help from someone else? The adult is bundled up in a cloak and both passengers are surrounded by a "shield" of those protective swords. They're making their getaway from trouble and as they do, they're safe. The boat is floating on a large body of water, which represents emotions, and it's moving from the choppy waters, or disruptive feelings, into smooth waters, or calmness and harmony. Rational thought is the protective force while moving through rough emotions into smoother ones.

If this card appears, then it's more useful to approach the emotional turbulence with clarity and logic. Step outside of your feelings and think your way through the issue. Come up with progressive solutions, rather than wallowing in the drama. Movement is key, and it's useful to consider whether your boat is still metaphorically tied to the dock in some way. If it is, untie the knots that are preventing you from moving forward into those smoother waters. It may even be time to use one of those sharp mental swords to cut ties altogether.

The idea of the ferryman is something we don't encounter in our modern-day world. Ferries are shuttles to take passengers across bodies of water, and in pre-industrial times, these ferries could sometimes be small boats to take passengers across lakes and even rivers that didn't have bridges, transporting them to lands that would otherwise be inaccessible. When we look at the Six of Swords, it's important to remember that the journey that you're on is one that is only accessible with the help of others. It's a team effort. You need others or they need you.

The most famous ferryman of all is Charon (pronounced like the name Karen). In Greek mythology, Charon was a particular sort of ferryman; he was a *psychopomp*—a guide who assisted the spirits of the newly dead on their trip to the afterlife. His role was to transport the spirit across the river Styx, from the world of the living to the world of the dead. When a person was buried in ancient Greece, a coin was placed in or on their mouths to pay the ferryman. When we see the Six of Swords, it's useful to reflect not only on the questions, where are you going and what are you leaving behind, but also, how are you going to pay the fare? It's time to examine your journey and set a course for where you want to go and determine how you're going to get there.

The Keys to the Treasure Chest— Key Symbols of the Six of Swords

Adult figure—the experienced self

Child figure—the intuitive self, the inner child

Distant land—goals and destinations, unknown territory

Ferryboat—floating above emotion, easy transport

Ferryman—the motivator, the guide, going back and forth, helping others

Passengers—moving from the known into the unknown with assistance

Pole—action, movement with energy and effort

Rough water—turbulent emotions

Smooth water—harmony, calm, peace, tranquil emotions

Swords—clarity in thought, thoughts over feelings, rationality protects

The Wizard's Words of Wisdom—
What the Six of Swords Signifies in a Reading

There is someone helping you as you make your way through life

Use your rational thought to move out of turbulent feelings

You are ready to untie your boat from the dock and embark on your journey

You help others move from emotional messes into peace

You move forward with the help of others

Behind the Mysterious Door—Journal Questions
to Explore the Six of Swords More Deeply

Where are you going? What do you need to leave behind?

Magic Words—Affirmation for the Six of Swords

"I am always moving toward a better future."

Your Adventure with the Seven of Swords

Seven of Swords

You look down on an encampment. Brightly colored tents are set up with banners waving in the breeze. Directly in front of you, a young man is stealthily sneaking away with five swords. He's looking back over his shoulder at the camp or perhaps at the two swords he is leaving stuck into the ground behind him.

The Seven of Swords shows a man who appears to be stealing swords from an enemy camp. On one hand, we could see this as a deplorable act. "Stealing is wrong," may be our immediate reaction, but what if there is more to the story? What if the guys he's stealing from are some really bad dudes and he's one of the good guys stopping them from slaughtering innocent people with those swords? What if he's just taking back what rightfully belongs to him? What if he's not stealing the swords from an enemy but playing a prank on some friends? Maybe he's not taking the swords at all, but merely rearranging them. One of the things that this card always awakens in the savvy reader is the idea that there may be more than one side to the story and that the way of the Trickster is to show us that things are not always what they appear to be.

The Trickster is an important archetype who appears in many different stories and mythologies. The Trickster is generally someone bright and clever who uses his knowledge to subvert order or uses the tools of power against an oppressor. Mischief makers, pranksters, rule breakers, whatever you want to call them, the Trickster figure is an important one. He is the one who "gets away with it." I see this Seven of Swords fellow as one of those Trickster figures. He's sneaking away with the swords and kind of doing it with a smirk. He knows he's outsmarting his opponents.

It's important to pay attention to the fact that this is a Swords card and thus is about thought and communication. This card is clearly about using a quick wit and silver tongue to get away with something. It can mean strategizing and planning something that you're going to get away with or using your wits on the fly to get the better of a situation. Or, alternatively, it can mean that someone is scheming and playing a mental chess game with you and it's a warning that you better be at the top of your own game. Likewise, when it comes to communication, it can mean you have powers of charm and flirtation to get what you want out of someone or that someone is using their charm on you.

The fact that this fellow is getting what he wants is something that is addressed energetically in the card. This is the "ask and you shall receive" card. It indicates that you have the power to ask the Universe, your lover, your potential lover, your boss, your mom, whoever, for what you want and get it. I also call this guy "the politician" or "the salesperson." All politicians want your vote and all salespeople want to make the sale, but a good politician or salesperson will listen and address the needs of the person she is focused on and turn up her powers of persuasion. Learn from these skilled influencers how to engage people so that they will want to give you exactly what you desire.

The Keys to the Treasure Chest—
Key Symbols of the Seven of Swords

Banners—order, group mentality

Distant soldiers—those who are unaware

Man holding five swords—craftiness, living by wits and persuasive communication

Red boots—hiding in plain sight, stealth

Red fez—divine connection, fearlessness

Tents—temporary circumstances

Two swords remaining—more work to do, leaving something behind

The Wizard's Words of Wisdom—
What the Seven of Swords Signifies in a Reading

Ask for it and you'll get it

Creatively subvert the system

Question authority

Use your powers of persuasion to get what you want

You can outsmart something or someone

Behind the Mysterious Door—Journal Question
to Explore the Seven of Swords More Deeply

What do I need to ask for and whom do I need to ask?

Magic Words—Affirmation for the Seven of Swords

"I am able to strategize to get what I want."

Your Adventure with the Eight of Swords

Eight of Swords

As you walk along a shoreline, you come across a woman who is tied up and immobilized. She stands still with her feet in a puddle at low tide. She is blindfolded and has some strips of cloth tying her arms to her side. She has a small fence of swords around her, three on her right and five on her left.

When this card appears, I've had clients say out loud, "That doesn't look good," but this is one of those cards that is actually quite helpful. This is a card about *perceived* limitations. The woman is standing immobilized, but if she would take off that blindfold, she could see that the wrappings that bind her aren't very tight and she could easily wriggle out of them. She would also see that the fence of swords doesn't completely encircle her and that there is only a shallow puddle at her feet. She stands there, frozen and passive, but in reality, with even a little awareness, she could easily escape what's entrapping her.

This card reminds me of a story. A person went to visit some elephants kept in captivity. These massive creatures were being held by thin ropes attached to a stake. When she saw this, she asked the trainer how this was possible, when these huge, powerful animals could easily break the rope or pull out the stake with just a yank. The trainer explained that when the elephant was small, it was attached to the same size rope, which was strong enough to hold a small elephant. It learned as a young baby that the rope would hold it, so it knew that pulling on the rope to escape was futile. As it grew, it never questioned that the rope could restrain it. When it reached powerful adulthood, it had "learned" that the rope would hold fast and never questioned that belief.

It's the same for us. Often we learn something through experience and then let that experience define us and our views of the world. In other words, our thoughts control us and we've allowed our experience to color those thoughts. This can show up in so many areas of our lives, but the one where these unhelpful beliefs seem to thrive most is in relationships. I'll see a client who is single and looking for love and if the Eight of Swords appears, it's our signal to dive into where erroneous beliefs have held the client captive like the woman in this card.

If you believe that "all men are cheaters," for example, then my follow-up question is, "Have you met all three billion males in this world and determined that they're all unfaithful?" There are many, many types of men out in the world and, yes, some of them are cheaters, but by holding the belief that *all* men are cheaters, you are bound to attract the ones that confirm that belief. What if, instead of holding that belief, we just say that there are some out there who are cheaters and some who are not and reserve judging anyone he's shown you who he is. After all, you wouldn't want him to have a belief about you because of something that his ex did to him.

Unravel the beliefs that are keeping you from moving forward toward finding love, getting your dream job, feeling good about your life. Start the process of removing the blindfold and bindings that are holding you back. If you believe only people with supermodel looks are deserving of love, for example, then you can be sure that you are holding an erroneous belief. You have to use a three-step process to uproot these beliefs.

1. Take off the blindfold. Assess your belief and determine if it is actually true. Have you only seen supermodels in love? Of course not. And have you seen beautiful people who are single or in troubled relationships? Yes. And have you seen people with less than perfect looks in great relationships? Of course you have.

2. Take off the bindings that tie you. Look for examples that disprove your belief. "Chris and Sam have an amazing relationship and, while they're my friends and I love them, I don't think anyone would say they look like supermodels."

3. Walk out of the fence of swords. Replace the constricting belief that was holding you bound with a new, open, expansive belief. "I am totally ready and worthy of having an amazing love come into my life."

By taking off your own blindfold, by wriggling out of the bindings that are holding you back, and by stepping out of the fence that your thoughts have created into an open field of possibility, you create the space for the magic to happen.

The Keys to the Treasure Chest—
Key Symbols of the Eight of Swords

Blindfold—not seeing the reality of the situation

Bound woman—constriction, stuck energy, holding back, binding yourself to your beliefs

Distant castle—beliefs that dreams and aspirations are too far and unattainable

Puddle—beliefs that emotions are shallow, intuition is not to be trusted

Swords stuck in the sand around her—thoughts and beliefs are blocking you

The Wizard's Words of Wisdom—
What the Eight of Swords Signifies in a Reading

Only your thoughts are blocking you

There are ways out of the mess you're in

You are allowing yourself to be controlled by limiting beliefs

You are freer than you believe yourself to be

You may not be seeing the whole picture

Behind the Mysterious Door—Journal Questions
to Explore the Eight of Swords More Deeply

How do my beliefs about a certain topic keep me from attracting the best things in life? What new expansive belief about this topic do I want to hold?

Magic Words—Affirmation for the Eight of Swords

"I open my mind and open the road to my success."

Your Adventure with the Nine of Swords

Nine of Swords

You step into a dark bedroom with nine swords mounted on its black walls. There is a person sitting up in bed with his face buried in his hands. A quilt lies over his legs; its brightly colored patches alternating with poppies and astrological symbols.

There is no doubt that this card reflects a challenge. Here we see an image of someone who is distraught and indulging thoughts that are creating stress, anxiety, and loss of sleep. It could be that this person has woken up from a nightmare and realized that the fear was all a creation of his mind. It could also be said that the person hasn't been able to sleep at all, with his thoughts keeping him awake at night.

Most people would look at the Nine of Swords and think, "Ugh! This is a terrible card! I don't want to get this in a reading," but like all the cards of the tarot, it holds the key to solutions. The person in the card is upset over something, but we see those nine swords floating in the background. Whatever he is worried about he has created in his own head, not an actual threat from outside. When we see this card, it's showing you that you are giving worry too much power over your life. Ninety-nine percent of the time, the thing we worry about never comes to pass. So worry is, at the very least, a waste of your precious time and, at the very worst, it's you putting your precious energy toward exactly what you don't want. Worry is letting your thoughts control you, rather than you being in control of your thoughts.

It's human nature to worry, but when the worry becomes habitual, ruins your sleep, or creates nightmares, you have let your mind take control, rather than being in charge of your mind. When this card appears, it's a wake-up call to look at your thoughts, recognize what you are worrying about, and replace those stressful thoughts with more helpful beliefs. Letting go is part of the process and the red poppies on the quilt are about that release. The astrological symbols on the quilt represent creating order out of the chaos that this worry creates and having mastery over what appears to be random. The carving on the side of the bed has a clue for us too. It shows one person vanquishing another. We can either be the victim, with our thoughts destroying our happiness, or we can choose to be the victor by banishing the worry, anxiety, and fears and replacing them with positive intentions and plans.

The Keys to the Treasure Chest—
Key Symbols of the Nine of Swords

Carving on bed—being either the victor over your thoughts or being vanquished by them

Figure sitting in bed—unnecessary worry, anxiety, stress, sleeplessness

Nine swords—overthinking, thoughts running out of control, ruminating

Quilt—comfort and protection comes from release of chaos and inviting in order

The Wizard's Words of Wisdom—
What the Nine of Swords Signifies in a Reading

Control your thoughts and control your destiny

Let go of the unhelpful beliefs you are holding about your situation

Relax and allow the results to unfold

Worry is a waste of time and energy

Your thoughts are running away with you

Behind the Mysterious Door—Journal Questions to Explore the Nine of Swords More Deeply

What unhelpful thoughts do you need to conquer? What will you tell yourself in place of the worried thought?

Magic Words—Affirmation for the Nine of Swords

"I am the master of my thoughts and I control my destiny."

Your Adventure with the Ten of Swords

Ten of Swords

At a shoreline, you see the body of a man face down in the sand. Ten swords are stuck into his back and a red cape mingles with the blood draining from his body. His hand rests by his side with two fingers making a sign of blessing. A black sky hovers overhead but beyond the horizon, dawn is breaking.

The Ten of Swords is a card that looks terrible if you don't look beyond the initially shocking image. The man is dead, there is no doubt about that. A guy with one sword stuck in his back might have a chance of being rushed to the emergency room and surviving, but a man with ten swords? He's saying, "Stick a fork in me, I'm done!" However, if we look off into the distance, we see a new day dawning. There is something new that is about to begin. This card is very black and white. When it shows up in a reading, you are absolutely closing one chapter and beginning a new one. For good or bad, there is no going back.

When the last chapter was something that we wanted to get rid of, the Ten of Swords can be a relief. We are closing the door on that tough time, opening up a fresh new chapter, and never ever have to go back to that struggle. But even if the last chapter was something that we thought we wanted, remember that the new chapter can be even better, if we just surrender to this ending and open up joyfully to our fresh, new beginning.

The Keys to the Treasure Chest—
Key Symbols of the Ten of Swords

Black night sky—"It's always darkest before the dawn," leaving darkness behind

Dawn—a new day dawning, a new chapter, freshness

Distant mountain shoreline—new adventures, new experiences ahead, overcoming challenges

Figure face down on the shore—finality, endings, you won't have to go back

Still body of water—calming the emotions, placidity, serenity, emotional territory to cover

Ten swords in his back—repeated messages of ending, thoroughness

Two fingers pointing—this ending is a blessing, possibly in disguise

The Wizard's Words of Wisdom—
What the Ten of Swords Signifies in a Reading

Being able to say, "You're done!"

Closing one chapter and opening a new one

Cutting ties with painful habits

Finishing things thoroughly

Never having to return to what you leave behind

Behind the Mysterious Door—Journal Question
to Explore the Ten of Swords More Deeply

What am I ready to let go of once and for all?

Magic Words—Affirmation for the Ten of Swords

"I move smoothly and effortlessly into my new, amazing chapter."

[8]

The Fun and Fiery Wands

now we step out of the world of thought into the world of action with the fiery Wands. At first glance, it may be difficult to see how we get the element of fire out of these wooden sticks. However, with just a little imagination, you can imagine these staffs as torches with their tops aflame and then it all seems to make sense.

While the Swords are meant to define and cut with the precision of clear thought and ideas, the Wands are the realm of action, passion, and will. When we go through the process of manifesting something, the first step is the idea (Air/Swords) while the next step is taking action on that idea (Fire/Wands).

Think about the essence of fire: it can be the warmth of a fireside, the light shed by a candle, or the raging destruction of a forest fire. When our ancient ancestors mastered the control of fire, it created a huge evolutionary shift for humans. It allowed them to live in colder climates and therefore expand their hunting territory. It let them cook their food and expand their diet. Fire was used in hunting, tool making, art, and extending the daylight hours with its artificial light. If you think about the correspondence of fire, when it comes to the Wands, it's all about the fire within: creativity, passion, action, and will. After the cool, cerebral quality of the metallic Swords, we have the fiery passionate Wands. As we dive into this suit, you'll get a flavor for what it means to be truly on fire.

Your Adventure with the Ace of Wands

Ace of Wands

You look over a pastoral scene. In the distance, beyond a grove and over a river, you see an impressive castle on a hill. From the sky above you, a grayish cloud descends with a hand emerging from it. The hand is holding a wooden staff upright. Small new branches with bright green leaves sprout out of the top and sides of the stick, while eight leaves flutter around it.

The Ace of Wands represents the pure essence of Wand energy: passion, excitement, energy, action, will, courage, and creativity. Aces also represent something new coming into the picture, just like that hand descending from above. There is also the message of all Aces: that the answer from Spirit is a "Yes"—especially if the topic is approached with passion, courage, and enthusiasm. With its knob at the top, some might say that the wand in the Ace resembles an Irish *shillelagh*; others might see the shape as something a little more phallic. And its purpose is a little ambiguous. Is it a club-like weapon or a magician's wand that is being handed to you?

Those new spring leaves sprouting everywhere represent the vitality and action of this card's energy. Fire is the life force. It's also a reminder that age really *is* just a number. You can see a young person who has had the fire go out of their soul and they don't compare at all to the octogenarian who lives life with a sense of wonder, eagerness, and adventure.

As we learned when looking at the similar Ace of Swords, the little leaves drifting down are actually yods in disguise—points of divine energy. This time, however, there are eight fluttering around the wand.

The number eight represents the momentum that comes from energy cycling on itself. Think of a figure eight and the continuous movement of the infinity symbol.

The river that we see in the middle ground also represents that movement: travel, change, and life rolling along. The castle in the distance represents a very sublime goal or aspiration. Something that you really, really want. While the distant hills and mountains represent the surmountable challenges that may lie ahead.

When the Ace of Wands makes an appearance in your reading, you're being handed an opportunity. Seize it with passion and you will have success.

The Keys to the Treasure Chest— Key Symbols of the Ace of Wands

Branches—new life, vitality, something sprouting up, vigor

Castle on the hill—future aspirations, big visions

Cloud—a spiritual message, passion burning through the haze

Distant mountains—future challenges are conquered through will

Eight leaves/yods—divine blessings raining down

Hand—something being handed over to you

River—movement, flow, action, change

Trees—growth, vitality

Wand—fire, new passion, enthusiasm, a burst of energy, starting an action

The Wizard's Words of Wisdom— What the Ace of Wands Signifies in a Reading

A "Yes" from the Universe

Being handed a magic wand that sparks your inner fire

Fresh passion, enthusiasm, and will

New or renewed sexual passion

Taking action toward attaining your big dreams

Behind the Mysterious Door—Journal Question to Explore the Ace of Wands More Deeply

What new passion am I ready to bring into my life?

Magic Words—Affirmation for the Ace of Wands

"I am on fire."

Your Adventure with the Two of Wands

Two of Wands

You stand at the battlement of a medieval castle behind a man who is dressed in the garb of a Renaissance explorer. He holds a staff in his left hand with a second staff bracketed to the stone parapet on his right. A beautiful painted cross, made of roses and lilies, decorates the stone wall to his left. In his right hand, he holds a globe as he gazes ahead at the land and sea below him.

The explorer in the Two of Wands is so engrossed with his vision that it seems as though he isn't even aware that we are standing behind him. I always imagine this card being one of the Spanish, Italian, or Portuguese explorers of the Renaissance. While the effects of their explorations were disastrous to the indigenous people of the Americas, when we look at the drive, ambition, and boldness behind their curiosity, those traits in their purest form are something we see reflected in this card. Imagine living in a time where many people believed that if you sailed out to sea, you might fall off the edge of the world! Then imagine rebelling against this belief and having the courage to go into completely unknown territory. These explorers had vision. "I'm going to be the first to find El Dorado." "I'll be the first to find an ocean route to India." "I'll be the first to sail around the world!" This is the essence of the Two of Wands: Vision.

Vision is beyond just dreaminess. It's having a dream, believing that it can be done, and then acting on that belief. Pioneers, inventors, explorers, and trailblazers all have this quality. And when you see this card show up in a reading, you know that it means to hold the vision of what you want and then act on that vision.

Our explorer in this card holds a globe in his hand as if to say,

"I can envision a new route to China," and he looks out over the sea making his plan for travel. He is determined; he knows that he can do it. That small globe is a representation of the larger world in front of him. The globe is the place where he can plan his adventure. It's the vision that he holds in his hand that allows him to say, "I got this!"

One staff is mounted with a bracket to the stony, solid parapet next to him. He has had visions in the past that he's turned into reality, and he's put those accomplishments up on the shelf and moved on. It's not that he's ignoring his past achievements, he's proud of them, but they don't hold his interest like the new lands that he is going to explore. However, his past successes have given him the confidence to start this new adventure.

While his red hat indicates that his intention may look like a material goal to the outside world, and may have been his original motivation, the rose and lily reflect that his mission embraces both material and spiritual goals. A question to ask when this card appears is, "What are the sacred aspects of this plan as well as the materialistic gain?" It's no problem if your vision includes both.

As with all of the Two cards in the Minor Arcana, he stands at a crossroads, do I choose this path or another one? Do I go forward or go back? The lily and rose cross to his left represents standing at that crossroads—literally the place where two roads meet, a place where magic happens. When this card shows up in a reading, you have the opportunity to make a magical decision. Most likely the decisions are, "Do I need to reflect more on this dream, or do I take action now to make that dream come true? Do I choose the path of the lily and focus just on the vision now or do I take the path of the rose and take a step into action?" There is no right or wrong answer here. Our explorer looking out to sea might be musing on this very issue. He's got his traveling cloak and boots on, so he's ready to go, but he's standing and reflecting, "Is now the right time to set sail or do I need to wait for better weather?" He's not abandoning his dream or holding back out of fear, there is always a forward momentum, but he's also being strategic about his action.

The village below him represents the fact that to gain what you want, you may have to leave the comfort of the familiar. This is echoed in the parapets around him. To venture out into new territory, he'll have to risk leaving the safety of his castle. He may meet challenges, represented by those distant mountains, but the calm sea in front of him means that there will be little emotional drama.

The Keys to the Treasure Chest—
Key Symbols of the Two of Wands

Cross—being at a decision point, choosing when to act

Explorer—courage, going into the unknown, discovering something new

Globe—visioning the possibilities, believing that "if you vision it, you can have it"

Lilies—incorporating a spiritual element into your vision

Mountains—challenges to be considered

Parapet—the safety and protection of the known

Red hat—material world accomplishments on one's mind

Roses—bringing a practical element to your vision

Sea—smooth sailing, a calm and steady path to your goals

Traveler's cloak and boots—prepared for the journey

Village—the comfort of the conventional

Wand in the bracket—past achievements and accomplishments

Wand in the hand—passion and enthusiasm for a new venture

The Wizard's Words of Wisdom—
What the Two of Wands Signifies in a Reading

Dare to dream big

Follow up vision with courageous action toward the goal

Formulate a new belief in the possibilities

Hold on to the highest vision of what can be

You've done it before, you can do it again

Behind the Mysterious Door—Journal Question
to Explore the Two of Wands More Deeply

What visions do I have for the future?

Magic Words—Affirmation for the Two of Wands

"If I can dream it, I can do it."

Your Adventure with the Three of Wands

Three of Wands

You stand at the edge of a high cliff, directly behind a merchant who is gazing out across the sea in front of him. He is dressed in the rich red robes of wealth and high rank and looks over at the three little ships that he's sending off to trade with a country far away. He authoritatively rests his right hand on a staff planted into the ground, while two additional staffs stand at his back. A black-and-white checked sash decorates his robe, which slips back and reveals the armor he's wearing underneath.

The man on the Three of Wands evokes cool confidence. He's got everything set up and now is putting his plans into motion. Like those black-and-white checks on his sash, this man knows how to play the chess game. He's a master strategist and he's thought through several steps ahead. Think about the stress of being a ship owner in the days before cell phones, Internet, and GPS. Once you sent your ships out and they went over the horizon, you would have no way of knowing if they would get hit by a storm, attacked by pirates, or your captain and crew would simply take off with your goods. A successful owner would not only have to be smart enough to strategically plan ahead as to what trading would bring him the biggest profit, but also to pick a trustworthy captain and crew, and have the calm confidence not to panic when his ships sail out of sight. He is certain that he has the best and most experienced at the helm. He knows that they will guide his ships to the distant land where his agents will exchange the goods he has on board for expensive silks and spices. He trusts them to do the work that will bring him a tidy profit once they come back home. He also has the patience to know that once he sends his ships out, they will come back.

Trust and patience are the essence of this card. This card is about the Universe conspiring behind the scenes to bring your best outcome. I compare it to going to see a play in a theater. When you arrive before showtime, you sit down in front of those red velvet curtains. If it's fifteen minutes until they open, from your point of view in the audience, there is nothing happening. However, behind that curtain, people are hustling around, moving scenery and furniture, laying out props, putting on costumes, warming up their voices and bodies, practicing their lines, and getting into place. You can't see it, but all that preparation is happening so that when that curtain goes up, "ta-da!" There's a show!

It's the same for the merchant. He doesn't see, and doesn't have any reason to see, the day-to-day details of the ship sailing over to the trading post. He just has to send them on their way and patiently await their return, knowing that he has done everything in his power to have a successful outcome. And when this card shows up in a reading, it's a reminder that you have sent your ships of intention, your action, your spells out there in a powerful and positive way; your work now is to be patient and trust that the Universe is setting up all your good stuff behind the scenes and that a big reveal is on the way.

The Keys to the Treasure Chest—
Key Symbols of the Three of Wands

>Armor—preparation, protection, strength, fortitude, confidence

>Checkerboard sash—master strategist, being able to think several steps ahead

>Circlet—connection to divinely ordained authority, being a chosen one

>Distant land—long-range plans, challenges are far off and distant

>Red robe—past success, being an achiever

>Sea—smooth sailing, physical distance, time and space

>Three ships—thought, feeling, and action sending out intention, steady movement

Two Wands behind—the Universe has your back on this

Wand in hand—steadiness, assuredness

The Wizard's Words of Wisdom— What the Three of Wands Signifies in a Reading

Be patient and relaxed

Believe that everything will unfold in perfect timing

Distant journeys and travel overseas are possible

Have trust that your good stuff is on the way

You've done the work, now wait for the outcome to come back to you

Behind the Mysterious Door—Journal Question to Explore the Three of Wands More Deeply

What things could the Universe be doing behind the scenes while I am waiting for my good outcomes?

Magic Words—Affirmation for the Three of Wands

"Everything is coordinating to bring me my best outcome."

Your Adventure with the Four of Wands

Four of Wands

You step into a scene outside of a castle just as a celebration is about to begin. A party is headed your way and you're right at the spot where the celebration will commence. Two of the celebrants are already waving at you with bouquets in their hands. They are dressed in festive togas and wearing flower crowns as they march up a path toward a flowery canopy supported by four staffs. Flowers appear to be everywhere—the grounds around the castle and under the bridges are all in bloom.

This is such a happy card, it's almost impossible not to get caught up in the excitement and fun that is just beginning. You're being welcomed and greeted with big waves from two of the partygoers that are dressed in their festive clothes. When you see a toga, it's natural to think Toga Party! There are definitely some fun times ahead.

When we see this card, it's about a celebration that has a communal feel. This is the whole village getting together to feast and have fun. In the context of relationship, this card often signifies a wedding or a public celebration of a couple's commitment. Those four posts in the foreground resemble a *chuppah*, the canopy at a Jewish wedding the couple stands beneath, which represents the home that they will build together. The bountiful flowers and fruits decorating this canopy and the rest of the party represent fertility, abundance, and growth. There is an interesting juxtaposition in this card as well. The wands represent passion and fire, while the number four represents stability. Isn't that what the romantic ideal is? Sexy, hot chemistry along with a rock-solid commitment to one another? It doesn't always mean a marriage in the legal sense, but it certainly indicates a committed connection of some kind, one that is publicly known and gets the stamp of approval by friends and family.

When we look at this card in contexts outside of relationships, it means public celebration and recognition of achievement. This card often shows up when awards are going to be given, and when the powers that be applaud your achievements and you receive pats on the back. This is a card reflecting acknowledgment of your efforts. You did a great job! Bravo!

There is a sense of attainment here. We've reached the top of whatever we were working to achieve. Now, we can relax and enjoy the fruits (and flowers) of our labor—but the celebration doesn't have to end. The bridge in the background indicates that this success will lead to future triumphs.

The Keys to the Treasure Chest—
Key Symbols of the Four of Wands

Bridge—reaching an achievement that becomes a starting point for something more

Canopy—a celebration, enjoying the fruits of your labor, establishing a happy home

Castle—future dreams are attainable and within reach

Flowers and fruits—sharing your abundance with others, effortless productivity

People celebrating—joyfully gathering with others, showing the world your happiness

Wands—long-lasting enthusiasm, passion leading to structure

The Wizard's Words of Wisdom—
What the Four of Wands Signifies in a Reading

Celebrating a group or community effort

Others celebrating your passionate and stable relationship

Receiving recognition from others

Recognizing something in your life worth celebrating

Showing others what you have accomplished

Behind the Mysterious Door—Journal Question to Explore the Four of Wands More Deeply

> What do I want to celebrate and how can I celebrate it with others?

Magic Words—Affirmation for the Four of Wands

> "I have so much to celebrate in my life."

Your Adventure with the Five of Wands

Five of Wands

As you're walking across a meadow, you come upon five young men on a rough patch of ground who are brandishing wooden staffs with bravado, clanking them against each other. One raises his wooden pole high in the air, another playfully pushes his against his friend, while another swings his over his shoulder.

What is happening in the image of the Five of Wands? Some people interpret this scene as one of serious fighting, but if you take a closer look at the clothes they are wearing, their rather casual stances, and their playful expressions, you can start to see that this doesn't look like a real fight at all. We've walked into a scene where a bunch of teenagers were sent out to accomplish the task of building something and ended up play fighting with these staffs. If you've ever been in charge of a group of kids, you know how the energy, passion, exuberance, and playfulness they have can bubble over into playful tussles and goofing around and then nothing gets done.

That's what we're seeing here: a bit of chaos, distraction, lack of leadership, basically unfocused energy gone haywire. The one on the far left is saying, "Ha ha! Got you!" to the guy in the center. The guy in the center looks back at lefty and says, "Come on, you guys, we're supposed to be building something with these." The one with the red tunic and the cap is hitting the staff of the guy in polka dots, while polka dots challenges him with an, "Oh yeah?" The kid on the far right looks as if he's ignoring everyone else, spacing out, looking up into the sky and saying, "If I start by putting my staff this way, we could attach them together. . ." They are all doing different things. One is trying to work, another is trying to organize, and the others are playing—there is no unity even in their fooling around and, most certainly, no progress is being made.

There is no doubt that the energy represented by this card is strong passion, action, and will, but it's strong will pulling in five different directions. When this card shows up in a reading, we are looking at this same kind of inefficient, time-wasting chaos in the air. If it's external, it represents an environment where no one is on the same page, people are at cross-purposes, and everyone is doing their own thing—they may even be working against one another. These are the kinds of work-places where everyone is running around chaotically or homes where no one in the family is helping anyone else. It doesn't have to be people who are creating the chaos though, it can also mean being pulled in too many different directions by demands in your life and getting nothing done. Sometimes this energy can even be found within, when we are distracted, working against our own best interests, confused, indecisive, or lacking focus.

This card looks like a hopeless situation. What the hell do we do when there is all this pandemonium around and we can't control the battling forces? There is an answer, and the clue isn't one that's easy to see. It's found in the clothing of the young men. Some of their articles of clothing are red, some are green, and then we have our friend in the polka dots. The red clothing represents the passion of that out of control energy that requires careful channeling. You don't want to put out the fire completely, after all you have to have action and energy to get your structure built, but you definitely have to get everyone moving in the same direction and focused on working together. The green of their clothing represents growth. Yes, these boys have to grow up, that's for sure, but it also represents that this situation hides within it an opportunity for growth. It may be that the struggles that you are sensing are really growing pains for the group—or your own growing pains, if the struggle is within. This conflict or disorganization has within it the opportunity for inner growth. It's not hopeless, and all this struggle isn't for nothing. You will gain something out of putting in the effort to find a solution here. Lastly, our fellow dressed in the polka dot clown costume reminds us not to take the situation too seriously. Lighten up. Find the humor in it all. Approach it with playfulness and you will diffuse any anger or aggression.

The Keys to the Treasure Chest—
Key Symbols of the Five of Wands

Green clothing—growth, gaining something from the experience

Polka dots—finding humor, lightheartedness, not taking the situation seriously

Red clothing—passion, energy, worldly concerns

Wands—passionate opinions and ideas, energy moving in different directions

Young men—inexperience, confusion, disorganization, lack of leadership

The Wizard's Words of Wisdom—
What the Five of Wands Signifies in a Reading

Being at cross-purposes

Confusion and distractions

Laughing at the absurdity of the situation

The necessity of focus

Struggles around you or within you

Behind the Mysterious Door—Journal Question
to Explore the Five of Wands More Deeply

What area of my life needs more focus and order?

Magic Words—Affirmation for the Five of Wands

"I rise above the chaos and focus my energy."

Your Adventure with the Six of Wands

Six of Wands

You stand in the middle of a parade. A man wearing a laurel wreath rides by you on a white horse carrying a wooden staff with another laurel wreath at the top. People are marching alongside him, waving wands in solidarity and celebration.

The Six of Wands depicts a "hail the conquering hero" moment. The rider is carrying and wearing a laurel wreath. In ancient Greece, the winners of athletic competitions, the best poets, and successful military leaders were crowned with laurel wreaths to symbolize their victory. So here comes our guy. He not only is *wearing* a laurel wreath, he's *carrying* one too! He's won more than once! When this shows up in a reading, you can expect victory in a competitive situation and perhaps in more than one area. You have enough success to share with those around you.

Our hero is riding in on a horse that is luxuriously decked out in the trappings and caparison of a horse returning from a high-class tournament. The elegant cape that the horse is decked out in was not just decorative, it was designed to protect the horse from arrows in battle and was usually embroidered with the heraldic symbols identifying the rider's noble heritage. This rider has the resources on tap, such as connections and money, to come out on top. Even his horse is special, as a white horse was considered in many cultures to be a magical being (think of the mythical Pegasus or unicorn). By extension, the hero is being honored by riding this special steed.

There are also people marching next to the hero cheering him on, meaning that whatever he accomplished is something that other people appreciate. In other words, there is an opportunity to gain a fan club. An important aspect of this card is gaining that recognition, getting renown for yourself or acclaim for your project. I call this card the "famous-ish" card. Not quite as immortal as the Sun card, but people around you are definitely appreciating what you do and want to be in your orbit.

There is an intoxicating element to all the adulation of the Six of Wands. When others tell us that we are amazing, it feels good. For people with healthy self-esteem, who like themselves, this bit of recognition can feel like a treat. But for those whose self-esteem is a little shaky, that validation from others can feel a little *too* good. It can be a little bit like a drug, fun to experience but you don't want to get addicted to the high. You need to tread carefully when handing over your power to other people to decide your worth. It can feel great when they love you, but what about when they are critical? This card is about finding that sweet spot where we can enjoy the recognition without becoming a slave to other people's opinions. The surest way to prevent this is to make sure that your heart is filled with self-love and a deep inner knowing that you are worthy whether others see it or not. The rider has the wand holding his laurel wreath of victory in his right hand and the reins of the horse in his left. He's celebrating but he still maintains control of his own destiny. He doesn't let the cheering distract him from his own sense of self-worth.

The Keys to the Treasure Chest— Key Symbols of the Six of Wands

Caparison and trappings—external resources and support

Crowd—supporters, validation, recognition

Laurel wreath on head—success is your divine right

Laurel wreath on staff—success in more than one area

Six wands—group passion, team spirit

Traveler's cape—navigating a long road to success

White horse—honor, magical blessings, giving credit to those who helped

The Wizard's Words of Wisdom—
What the Six of Wands Signifies in a Reading

In a win-lose scenario, you will be the winner

Others will applaud your success

You will gain the admiration of others

You will succeed in your quest

Your achievement is also beneficial for the group

Behind the Mysterious Door—Journal Questions
to Explore the Six of Wands More Deeply

What accomplishment do I feel most proud of? What would I like to accomplish in the future?

Magic Words—Affirmation for the Six of Wands

"I am worthy of positive attention from others."

Your Adventure with the Seven of Wands

Seven of Wands

A young man, in a defensive stance, positions himself at the top of a hill with a staff poised to fend off all comers. The ground he stands on looks almost like distant mountains, as if he were a giant. He is dressed in a plain green tunic over a yellow shirt and brown leggings. He has a boot on his left foot and an unlaced shoe on his right. His face is fixed in an aggressive and focused gaze at the challenge he is facing. Below him, six wands are raised by unseen challengers attempting to knock him down from his advantageous position.

Whenever this card comes up in a reading, a few analogies come to mind—first, the game King of the Hill. If you ever played this game, you'll know that the basic premise is that one child is on top of a hill and the others try to knock him or her off so they can be the new King of the Hill.

The other image that comes up for me is the legend of Robin Hood and the story of how he met his future friend, Little John. They meet for the first time, while crossing over a fallen log bridge in opposite directions. Robin wants to go forward, but Little John won't let him—refusing to give way, because *he* wants to go in the opposite direction. They agree to take up staffs just like our fellow in the Six of Wands and, using those weapons, fight over who has the right to cross. The fight goes back and forth, but eventually Little John knocks Robin Hood off the bridge. Robin calls his band of Merry Men, who want to gang up on this rude man who has disgraced their leader, but Robin calls them off. Recognizing that it might be better to have a strong giant of a man as an ally, rather than an enemy, Robin invites John to join their band.

In the Seven of Wands, we see the echoes of these two concepts. A guy, standing on top of a hill, is fighting off the people who are trying to knock him down. He uses the staff to defend his position. That's what this card is about: standing strong, defending what's yours, and not backing down.

This guy is someone for whom defense is the first priority. He looks as if he just rolled out of bed, threw on a tunic, and grabbed the first two shoes he could find to get out there and fight for his rights, his property, his position. He's not geared up in armor—that would take too long. He doesn't have an army backing him up; there's no time to gather everyone together. All on his own, he fights to retain what belongs to him. I have the *right* to cross this bridge and you can't make me go backward. I *am* the king of this hill and you are not.

How did he get to that position on top of the hill? Well, clearly it's a sought-after place. I mean, everyone else wants to be up there. So, he had to put in the effort to get there in the first place. To get to the top, you gotta climb your way up there. The yellow of the man's shirt represents the good fortune he experienced and the green of his tunic represents the growth that took place on his journey; it doesn't necessarily mean clawing your way up. Think of how mountain climbers make their way to the top of a mountain. There is definitely an element of luck, I mean you want to have great weather and avoid the snowstorms, but the effort you put in is equally important. To get to the peak, there is sacrifice and sometimes even danger. But a mountain climber doesn't ask to be dropped off at the top of the mountain by a helicopter. Part of the exhilaration of the experience is the journey and the effort it takes to get there.

So, when we see the Seven of Wands show up in a reading, it can be about any of these points. Maybe you are ambitious and focused, determined to make your way up to the top. Maybe you are courageously defending your hard-won gains against challenges that are coming at you. The fact that we can't see who's holding those wands is a reminder that those challenges are not always other people. With the focus that you have on getting to or staying at the top, you pay no mind to other people's opinions. So what if your shoes don't match! Keep your eyes on the prize and resist!

The Keys to the Treasure Chest—
Key Symbols of the Seven of Wands

Green tunic—continued growth, life force

Hill—you've climbed to this place, your position, your hard-won gains, your truth

Mismatched shoes—not concerned with what others think, quirky independence

Stance of the man—defending what you believe in, standing strong

Wand in hand—using your passion, action, and energy to climb the mountain and defend your stakes

Wands below—thoughts, people, or things that tell you "No," mindless opposition

Yellow shirt—luck is on your side

The Wizard's Words of Wisdom—
What the Seven of Wands Signifies in a Reading

Defend yourself from those internalized beliefs and external messages that contradict your truth

Don't back down

Fight for your rights

Put in the energy and effort to get to the top of your mountain

You be you

Behind the Mysterious Door—Journal Question
to Explore the Seven of Wands More Deeply

What am I willing to fight for?

Magic Words—Affirmation for the Seven of Wands

"I believe in me."

Your Adventure with the Eight of Wands

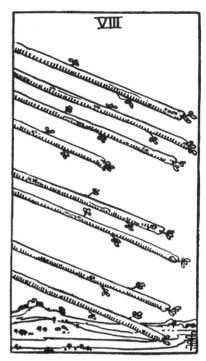

Eight of Wands

You look out at the landscape in front of you. A beautiful, clear, blue river flows across the scenery and verdant green hills rise gently at the horizon. If you look carefully, you can even see a white castle at the top of the highest hill, nestled among some lush trees. All of a sudden, eight wooden staffs go whizzing past you, flying in unison like javelins zooming toward a single target.

This card is one of the more befuddling ones of the Minor Arcana. There are no people or animals in it to give a sense of the scene. When you're just discovering this card for the first time, you may have to sit with it for a bit to get the essence of what's going on. Imagine that you are looking at eight arrows instead of eight wands and that they are all flying in unison toward a bull's-eye. Wands represent action, and here we see all actions focused toward a single goal. Just like an arrow flying through the air, there is no resistance to you reaching that objective. Things will move quickly without bumps in the road. However, there's an important thing to emphasize here: *all* the action is focused on the one goal. There are no distractions. There is no multitasking going on.

There's something more to this card too. In the description that Waite gives to the Eight of Wands, he tacks on at the end, almost as an afterthought, ". . . also the arrows of love." What happens when we fall in love? All we can think of is the object of our affection. No matter what else is going on in our life, we keep thinking of that person. Everything is a sign. We are reminded of them everywhere we go. We can't wait till the next chance we get to see them again. We lust after them. We want to be with them all the time. That's the kind of focus this card represents.

It *can* show up as love, but it can also show up as being really driven in your career, having a spiritual calling, wanting to get a degree, or becoming completely enthralled with a hobby. Wherever it has channeled, it feels like a mission. I think of that scene from *The Blues Brothers* movie, where Dan Aykroyd's character says, "We're on a mission from God." No matter what bizarre adventures ensue, the Blues Brothers *are* going to get the band back together and they're going to play. That kind of focus is what the Eight of Wands asks for, and in return it promises that the road to get to the goal will be open, smooth, and swift.

The Keys to the Treasure Chest— Key Symbols of the Eight of Wands

Castle—larger goals may seem distant but you are taking your steps to get there

New budding leaves—life force and passion blossoming

River—consistent movement

Rolling hills—obstacles are distant and minimal, if they exist at all

Wands flying through the air—focused energy and intention going toward a single goal

The Wizard's Words of Wisdom— What the Eight of Wands Signifies in a Reading

All will move quickly toward your goal

Everything will go smoothly

Gather your resources and send them in one direction

Put your attention on one project at a time

You are focused on your mission

Behind the Mysterious Door—Journal Question to Explore the Eight of Wands More Deeply

What is my first (or next) step to accomplish my mission?

Magic Words—Affirmation for the Eight of Wands

"Everything comes together quickly with grace and ease."

Your Adventure with the Nine of Wands

Nine of Wands

You come upon a man with a bandaged head standing behind a barricade made up of staffs stuck into the ground. He leans against one staff, holding it at the ready in case there is an attack. And he's ready for *any* potential onslaught, warily looking off to the side in case a band of marauders tries to sneak by his barricade.

One of the most helpful ways to really connect with your tarot deck is to create some made-up stories about the cards. Some of the tarot cards just seem to jump out with backstories and the Nine of Wands is one of those. Here we see someone who has been through some kind of trauma—he's got a bandage on his head, so we know he's had something happen to him in the past. And he's looking off to the side with a watchful expression. He's definitely expecting something to happen soon but whatever it is, he's going to be ready this time.

The bandage on his head is significant. According to Louise Hay, author of *You Can Heal Your Life*, the places where we feel pain or have an injury have correspondences to unhelpful beliefs that we hold about ourselves. This bandage on the head indicates that whatever we have been through has affected our thoughts and beliefs. Letting our experiences color our perceptions happens to even the best of us. We have a relationship with a cheater and then are fearful that our new love will cheat on us, too. We had an employee who stole from us and now we watch for shady behavior in all our employees. This card always brings to my mind the song "Won't Get Fooled Again" by The Who or that old saying: "Fool me once, shame on you. Fool me twice, shame on me." If we allow ourselves to be doormats, we have no one to blame but ourselves. There is definitely something strong about standing up for yourself and being ready for anything, but we have to look deeply and objectively within and determine if we are assessing the threats realistically or just reacting to our past trauma.

Nines represent the culmination of your action and reaching your goal. Here we have a guy who has nine wands. He's there! He has the safety of being behind a barricade but he still doesn't trust the world around him. He's a survivor but he doesn't believe in himself. I often say this card tells us that we have everything that we need to succeed (the barricade, we survived), but are still doubting ourselves (the wary glance, the ready weapon). Since so much of this card is emotional, it often shows up in a reading when self-esteem issues are sabotaging the situation. So, take a step back, look at how your self-doubts or doubts about the world may be coloring your viewpoint, and then recalibrate with a more trusting, open heart.

The Keys to the Treasure Chest— Key Symbols of the Nine of Wands

Bandage on head—mentally carrying old wounds

Distant mountain chain—the perception of challenges all around

Eight wands standing—you have everything you need to succeed, you are safe

Wand being held—you have resources to get you through

Wary gaze—well prepared, overly watchful, waiting for the other shoe to drop

The Wizard's Words of Wisdom— What the Nine of Wands Signifies in a Reading

Old history is coloring your perception of the situation

Self-esteem issues are being activated

Trust that you have the necessary resources

You are a survivor

You have everything that you need to succeed but you're doubting yourself

Behind the Mysterious Door—Journal Questions to Explore the Nine of Wands More Deeply

What experiences from my past may be coloring my present beliefs? What positive belief would I rather hold?

Magic Words—Affirmation for the Nine of Wands

"I have everything I need to succeed."

Your Adventure with the Ten of Wands

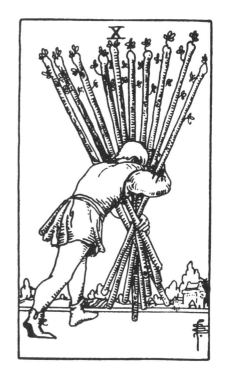

Ten of Wands

A man is walking toward a chateau in the distance. He is struggling to carry a bundle of ten staffs in his arms. He is so bent over with the burden that his head is buried in the bundle. Somehow, he's managing to move them, but it is taking a lot of effort and struggle.

Since Wands represent the element of fire, we can view this card as the card of impending burnout. The fellow in this card is clearly burdened with too much. He's gotten too enthusiastic about too many projects, taken them all on, and now feels overwhelmed. In fact, with his head stuck in his bundle, he can't even see his way out of the situation.

When this card shows up in a reading, one of the things that it addresses is the power in being able to delegate. Think about this: this guy is struggling with these ten staffs. He's getting them where they need to go, but there's no fun in this journey. If he asked for help and got someone else to carry five while he carried the other five, this would be a very different scenario. So, when this card appears, it's time to check in and assess what responsibilities can be shared with others. This card also asks us to take a look and see if we are being a bit of a martyr, willingly taking on the weight of the world, and then groaning under the burden of it all. Either way, it's time to cut back on some of our obligations before we suffer some physical, mental, or spiritual exhaustion.

To avoid finding yourself overcommitted and on the verge of burnout, the entrepreneur Derek Sivers recommends taking a beat before investing your time and energy into something. When reflecting on whether to say "yes" or "no" to another responsibility, he says that if the answer isn't a resounding "Hell, yeah!!" then the answer should always be "no." Think about it. If you are asked to make cupcakes for the school bake sale and your answer is not "Hell, yeah!" then it's a "no." If you are wondering if you should go back to school and get a degree, if you don't feel the "Hell, yeah!" then it's a "no." If you meet someone and they ask you to go out, if your answer is not "Hell, yeah!" then it's a "no." Think of how freeing up all that time and energy of not having to do things out of obligation can be channeled back into those few things that are the "Hell, yeahs!" Putting more of ourselves into the things that we love will create a life that is rich, juicy, and full of fun. Exactly how life is supposed to be.

The Keys to the Treasure Chest— Key Symbols of the Ten of Wands

Bent over man—unnecessary struggle, weight of the world on you

Bundle of staffs—impending burnout, too many irons in the fire, taking on too much

Chateau—material responsibilities

Head buried in the bundle—not being able to see your way out

The Wizard's Words of Wisdom— What the Ten of Wands Signifies in a Reading

A danger of impending burnout

Burning the candle at both ends

Saying "yes" when you should say "no"

Taking on more than your share of the responsibility

The need for less "I can do this all by myself," and more "Can you help me?"

Behind the Mysterious Door—Journal Question to Explore the Ten of Wands More Deeply

Where in my life are there obligations that I can share with others?

Magic Words—Affirmation for the Ten of Wands

"I make choices that free up more energy for the things that I love."

[9]

The Watery Depths
of the Cups

When we look at the cycle of manifestation, it starts first with the inspired idea of the airy Swords, then gets activated by the fiery Wands, and then moves into the realm where heart and soul are put into what we're creating and we invite the Universe to co-create with us. We dive into an adventure in the watery world of the Cups. It's easy to see where Cups correspond to the element of water. Water itself flows to fill in whatever space surrounds it, so the Cup is what holds water together. Water represents those parts of us that seem to come from that inner vessel: spirituality, intuition, and psychic awareness. The Cup is the center of the heart.

Cups are also the domain of certain emotions as well. While Wands represent outward, passionate, expressive emotions, Cups encompass the world of what I call the inward emotions—dreamy, poetic feelings that we may keep to ourselves more often than we share them with others. For example, both Wands and Cups can represent happiness, but for the Wands the expression of that would be shouting "Yay!" and for the Cups it would be a happy sigh and a mysterious smile. Wands can represent fiery, sexual passion, while Cups represent romance and falling in love. When Cups show up in a reading, you are looking into the interior life, deep emotion, mystic realms, psychic intuition, spiritual domains—all that stuff that happens inside of us. So, let's dive down deep and see what the watery depths have to show us.

Your Adventure with the Ace of Cups

Ace of Cups

You stand in front of a rippling pond, lush with water lilies and blossoming lotuses. A single cloud hovers in a gray sky. A hand emerges from this cloud, holding a golden chalice inscribed with what appears to be the letter *W*. The chalice has fountains spouting from it and shimmering little droplets raining down. A white dove descends toward the chalice holding a communion wafer impressed with an equal-armed cross.

The seemingly simple and straightforward Ace of Cups is a card full of riddles and puzzles. First off, we can start with the cup itself. For medieval English history buffs, or people who watch Monty Python movies, the symbolism seems obvious. The ornate chalice being handed down from a heavenly hand is reminiscent of the Holy Grail. Finding the Holy Grail, the cup Christ used at the Last Supper, was the quest of the Knights of the Round Table. This was no ordinary cup. The people searching for it believed that it had mystical powers to create miracles, grant eternal youth, or open the soul to infinite happiness. In several occult systems, the chalice also represents feminine energy. Many scholars of Celtic history believe that the search for the Holy Grail actually derives from pre-Christian motifs of magic cauldrons—those big black iron pots that blend and transform materials, but also create and make, much like a woman's womb creates a baby from a single sperm and egg. The symbol of a chalice is pure mystery and pure magic! And that's what the Cups represent. All the messy, yummy, hard-to-define spiritual alchemy that's created deep within.

As with all the Aces, we have a magical, benevolent hand delivering the pure essence of the element of water, flowing out of the cup in five delicate fountain-like streams and twenty-six shimmering yod-shaped droplets. The number five represent the human experience—our five fingers on each hand and our five senses, and so our soulfulness is connected to our experience in a human body in the physical world. Five also represents the four elements plus the fifth one, the mystical element ether. Ether was what classical Greek scientists and medieval alchemists called the material that fills space, and what more magical ones would call Spirit.

The yods are similar to ones we see scattered throughout the tarot representing divine blessings raining down, but the Ace of Cups wins the "Overachiever Award" in this category with the biggest number of them represented. Does it mean more blessings? Well, with the Cups representing that connection to the soulful and spiritual side, you wouldn't be out of line drawing that connection. Twenty-six is also two times thirteen, that magical witchy number. There are thirteen lunar cycles in a year and the mysterious moon that appears and disappears each month echoes the elusive nature of spirituality and psychic phenomena. The water from the streams and droplets is flowing into a still pond filled with lotuses and water lilies. These flowers symbolize regeneration and rebirth in spite of challenges.

The chalice itself is inscribed with what appears to be a *W* but, looking a little closer, it seems that the font is a bit off. What we're actually looking at is an upside down letter *M*. Many scholars believe that this is a reference to the Virgin Mary, mother of Jesus. The *M* is upside down to receive the Eucharist wafer that the Holy Spirit is placing inside. If we really want to dive into this Christian symbology, we can reference Matthew 1:18 which says that ". . . [Mary] was found to be pregnant through the Holy Spirit," and Luke 1:33-34 which says, "How can this [pregnancy] be," Mary asked the angel, "since I am a virgin?" The angel replied, "The Holy Spirit will come upon you. . ." So, when we are looking at that dove placing that "body of Christ" wafer into the womb-like chalice, what are we looking at here? Oh, just the moment of Jesus's conception. Talk about your magical vessels!

So, the message of the Ace of Cups in a reading is to connect with new soulfulness. This can mean new love opening your heart—a new romance, a new friend, a new baby, or a new pet, for example. Or it can mean that a new opportunity of another kind, one that brings fulfillment at the heart level, is being handed to you. It can also indicate that new spiritual or psychic insights open up for you. Regardless of whether the meaning is love, fulfillment, spiritual awakening, or psychic insight, the result is a filling of the heart and the conception of something deeply and personally meaningful to you.

The Keys to the Treasure Chest—
Key Symbols of the Ace of Cups

Chalice—cauldron of conception, emotions, dreams, psychic awareness, newness

Clouds—messages from above, emergence from mystery

Distant land—bringing spiritual experiences to the material world at some distant point

Dove—the Holy Spirit, life force, Spirit, awakening

Equal-armed cross—the meeting of the spiritual and material worlds

Eucharist—sacredness, internalizing divine energy, holy mysteries

Five streams of water—processing what you receive through the senses with Spirit

Hand—a divine gift, something being handed to you,

Pond—"still waters run deep," calm, feeling at peace in the world of emotion

Water droplets—divine blessings, nourishing spiritual rain, emotions bringing blessings

Water lilies and lotuses—regeneration, rebirth, transforming muck into beauty

The Wizard's Words of Wisdom—
What the Ace of Cups Signifies in a Reading

A "Yes" from the Universe

A new lover, friend, or family member

Connection to the domain of Spirit

Dreams and flashes of psychic intuition that lead to awareness

Manifestation driven by the magical ethereal element of soul

Behind the Mysterious Door—Journal Questions to Explore the Ace of Cups More Deeply

What new intuitive insights do I need to listen to? How am I opening my heart?

Magic Words—Affirmation for the Ace of Cups

"My heart is open to giving and receiving love on all levels."

Your Adventure with the Two of Cups

Two of Cups

You come across a man and a woman who are meeting outside. Each of them holds a golden goblet out toward the other. She's wearing a laurel wreath on her head and he's wearing a crown of red roses. He steps forward, reaching out to her tenderly. Between them hovers the head of a red winged lion over a *caduceus*, a staff with two snakes entwined around it. Off in the distance, you see rolling green hills with a little red-roofed house nestled among the trees.

One look at these two gazing into each other's eyes and you'll know that this card is about connection. The traditional description of this card is of "pledging" to one another, but beyond a pledge of duty, this is a pledge that is coming from a bonding of the hearts, a beautiful feeling of desire to commit in some way to someone else. Of course this can mean a romantic love, but it can also mean a commitment to a friend, family member, or work partner. Regardless of what or whom you are committing to, it comes from a place of open, heartfelt goodness and has a "you complete me" dynamic to it.

However, we don't want to water down the chemistry that's depicted between these two. We have all been in the presence of two lovers who are completely enraptured with one another, gazing into each other's eyes and blocking out the rest of the world just as these two are. That winged red lion represents that magical chemistry of passion (the lion) and spiritual connection (the wings) that magnetically draws us toward one another. Beneath the lion, floats the caduceus with those two intertwining snakes. Many people mistakenly associate the caduceus with doctors and medicine, but it's actually a symbol of the Greek god Hermes, representing communication, commerce, and messages. That communication back and forth between the two lovers builds the connection between them much like the energy of those two snakes wrapping themselves around the sexually suggestive rod. Even the shapes that those snakes make are reminiscent of a stylized vulva. You didn't realize this card was so hot, did you?

The woman is wearing a laurel wreath of victory while he wears a crown of red roses representing passionate love. I love that she is the one wearing this laurel wreath. He's in love and recognizes her accomplishments and she sees herself as a winner. Maybe winning his love was the real victory here. She wears blue and white, representing the high vibration spiritual feelings that we get when we become enraptured, while his yellow tunic and tights are symbolic of the bright open happiness we feel when we fall for someone. He's stepping forward while she stands still, representing the active and receptive, give-and-take qualities of truly loving partnerships. That little house in the distance represents a future of domesticity and building a life together, while the rolling green hills represent the ability to navigate the little ups and downs of life with ease.

When this card shows up in a reading, the connection between you and someone else is at the heart level. There is an understanding between you two that needs no words to communicate. The man and woman are gazing at each other as though there is no one else in the world, so this signifies the unique and magical nature of this connection. It's as if there is no relationship as amazing as yours. With focus and attention, you are able to take this beautiful love to a deeper spiritual level.

The Keys to the Treasure Chest—
Key Symbols of the Two of Cups

Blue and white robes—high vibration emotion, spiritual connection

Caduceus— communication creates connection, sexual intimacy

Laurel wreath—success, victory, recognition of your achievements by the other

Man and woman—partnership, loving emotion, romance

Rose wreath—passionate and ardent true love, the mind is on love

Two cups—deep feelings between two people

Winged lion—sensuality blended with spiritual connection, a higher form of passion

Yellow tunic and tights—happiness, positive feeling, and communication

The Wizard's Words of Wisdom—
What the Two of Cups Signifies in a Reading

Communication between two people opens up deeper positive feelings

Magnetic attraction and love blossom

Promises are beneficial for both parties

The connection to another has heartfelt feelings

Those you are connected with have your best interests at heart

Behind the Mysterious Door—Journal Questions
to Explore the Two of Cups More Deeply

Who opens their heart to me? What can I do to cultivate a deeper spiritual connection?

Magic Words—Affirmation for the Two of Cups

"I open my heart to connect meaningfully to others."

Your Adventure with the Three of Cups

Three of Cups

You're invited to an outdoor gathering where three lovely ladies are dancing together and toasting each other with golden goblets raised. They sway to the music amid the abundant fruits at their feet and wear bountiful flower crowns on their heads.

There's a party going on right here! These women are having a good time and some delicious wine is surely involved. The fruits around them are a tip off that they are celebrating a successful and abundant harvest. Of course, in our modern times, we *might* celebrate the abundance of a good harvest, but more likely we're celebrating a raise, a promotion, a successful project, or the expansion of a family. The three women together indicate a communal component, interacting with others in a fun social environment. Light, fun friendships and genuine camaraderie are highlighted. There's also a "let down your hair" or "lighten up" quality to this card. You don't need a reason to celebrate. Life is meant to be joyful and fun. The Cups are about emotion, and when this card shows up, it's an indication of emotions that are festive and light and connections to others that are playful and harmonious. The fact that there are three participating has an interesting feel to it as well. They are connecting to one another. It's not two forming a cozy friendship and leaving one out. This is a card of companionship and enjoyment being multiplied by the group in a "more the merrier" way. However, unlike the Four of Wands, which shows the whole village reveling, this celebration in this card has the intimate feel of getting together with close, loving friends and family. It's less about the public recognition and more about the shared joy.

The wine cups and that bunch of grapes in the hand of the woman on the right are reminiscent of the worship of Dionysus in ancient Greece or Bacchus in the Roman Empire. These were the gods of wine and their religious rites were typically spent imbibing their favorite drink freely. So, when this card appears, it indicates social activity that has that freewheeling quality. The one partygoer's red robes symbolize willingly enjoying the sensual pleasures, while the woman in white indicates that the reasons for the indulgence are positive and spiritually of a high vibration. The third woman in brown is that friend who is the designated driver, the one who takes care of the practical matters so that everyone gets home safe. She still has fun but makes sure things don't get out of hand.

The Keys to the Treasure Chest—
Key Symbols of the Three of Cups

Dancing—lightheartedness, play, fun, grace

Flower crowns—minds on abundance and happiness

Fruits—abundance, growth, success, raises, promotions

Three cups—hearts connecting in love and friendship, celebration, drinking

Three women—friendship, social activity, cooperation, camaraderie, equality

The Wizard's Words of Wisdom—
What the Three of Cups Signifies in a Reading

Friendship and warm closeness

Sharing joy with others

Highlight on social activity

Celebrating successes

Time to relax, have fun, and play

Behind the Mysterious Door—Journal Questions to Explore the Three of Cups More Deeply

What can I do to bring more play into my life? What can I celebrate today?

Magic Words—Affirmation for the Three of Cups

"I have so much to celebrate in my life."

Your Adventure with the Four of Cups

Four of Cups

You come to a small, grassy hill with a shady tree at the top. You see a young man dressed in a red shirt, blue tights, and a green tunic sitting against the tree trunk with his arms and legs crossed. He is looking at three golden cups in front of him, while off to the side a small cloud with a hand emerging from it holds a fourth chalice.

Have you ever been so obsessed with the daily issues in your life that you missed out on seeing the magic around you? It happens to the best of us. We get so caught up in getting to the destination that we forget to experience the joy of the journey. The fellow in this card is so focused on the everyday cups in front of him that he's missing out on the divine gift being presented just to his right. This card reminds us to be present, awake, and in the moment. If we are, we will have access to the magical synchronicities that are waiting for us.

Since this is a Cups card, it focuses on our inner emotional life. He's looking a little morose or at least bored. His arms are crossed in front of his chest as if to protect his heart. That posture and those three cups that he's focusing on represent being so fixated on the "real world" that he has become closed off to the magical world of the heart. It's as the author Antoine de Saint-Exupéry says in his book *The Little Prince*, "It is only with the heart that one can see rightly; what is essential is invisible to the eye."

It can also mean that we are overindulging in our emotions, those times that we latch on to the ego-centered idea that our hurt/sad/bad feelings are the most important thing. Have you ever been so hooked on your negative emotion that you couldn't enjoy something that would normally give you pleasure? When we put our attention on those self-indulgent feelings, we are more likely to miss out on the cup offered by the Universe that is filled with something that is going to make our hearts happy—love, fulfillment, joy. The message of the Four of Cups is to open up to the opportunities for happiness that exist all around us every day. Look for things to appreciate. Find your center again by finding things to be grateful for. Be a joy hunter.

The Keys to the Treasure Chest—Key Symbols of the Four of Cups

Arms and legs crossed—closed off to the new, protecting the heart

Cup being held by hand in a cloud—magical offerings that bring fulfillment

Distant rugged mountain peaks—potential challenges to face

Grassy hill—gentle support

Three cups on the ground—emotional ties to average things

Tree—being rooted by your habits, beliefs, or tradition

Young man with pensive expression—focusing on mundane issues

The Wizard's Words of Wisdom—What the Four of Cups Signifies in a Reading

Be aware that there are other options; be awake to see unlimited possibilities

Divine gifts are being offered to you

Focus less on the mundane tasks of living so that you can see the magic

Notice where you are putting your attention

Self-absorption will lead to missing out

Behind the Mysterious Door—Journal Questions to Explore the Four of Cups More Deeply

Where is my focus right now? How can I wake up to alternate perspectives?

Magic Words—Affirmation for the Four of Cups

"There is so much in my life to appreciate."

Your Adventure with the Five of Cups

Five of Cups

A black-cloaked figure stands on a road looking down sorrowfully at three cups that are knocked over. Red and green liquids are spilled at his feet. Behind him, two cups are standing upright. In the middle distance, a bridge crosses over a flowing river and connects to a gentle slope. And in the far distance, a fortress stands, surrounded by trees.

It is easy to see the emotions contained in this card: sadness, regret, pessimism. Although we're looking at cups that are spilled, I often call this the "glass half empty" card. The guy is looking sorrowfully at his spilled cups on the left and missing the upright cups on the right. The left represents the past and indicates that there is nothing that can be done to change the situation, but the right represents the future, and the message is one of hope, if you turn your attention toward what's to come.

There is something surprising in those spilled cups as well. We see the red wine that resembles spilled blood, but we also see a mysterious green liquid in the foreground. Whenever we see green liquids in old-time movies, we are looking at the shorthand for poison—think of the bubbling green toxic potions in a mad scientist's lab or a witch's cauldron. While the person is ruing his loss, what he may not have noticed is that this little bit of bad luck may have saved him from a complete catastrophe. I mean when the stakes are losing two glasses of good wine and not losing your life on that third glass of poison, the sacrifice seems worth it. Those cups are pointing away from him, indicating that he was the one to knock them over. Whether this happened because he was careless or he did it in a fit of rage, he can be confident that ultimately that little loss prevented an even greater one.

That bridge in the background to his right represents finding a bridge from the feelings of grief to the hopeful potential of the upright cups. Those cups may or may not have any wine in them, but the potential is there for a much happier outcome. We may have to do the work to fill them, but they're not knocked over in the dirt. If we have a sense of gratitude for the good things we have in our life, then our cups are more than filled. The flowing river represents change and movement. Whatever regret we're feeling right now won't last and the day will come again where we're feeling better. The fortress in the distance stands for eventually finding our way to the protection that we may crave in this situation.

The Keys to the Treasure Chest— Key Symbols of the Five of Cups

Black cloak—grieving, hiding in a protective cocoon, wrapping oneself in sadness

Bridge—moving through grief to happiness, crossing over the emotional waters

Figure with bowed head—sadness, remorse, regret, reflecting on the past, feeling loss

Fortress—finding our way to shelter and protection

River—change, movement, life going on

Three spilled cups—loss of something desirable along with the loss of something detrimental

Two upright cups—potential for something positive in the future

The Wizard's Words of Wisdom— What the Five of Cups Signifies in a Reading

Allow yourself to grieve, then let it go

Decide for yourself what you will fill your future cups with

Don't let the past define your future

Focus on what you have, not what you've lost

Realize that a small loss may have prevented a greater one

Behind the Mysterious Door—Journal Question to Explore the Five of Cups More Deeply

What past loss am I ready to leave behind?

Magic Words—Affirmation for the Five of Cups

"I open myself to a brighter future."

Your Adventure with the Six of Cups

Six of Cups

On a village lane, a little boy gives a little girl a golden goblet with a white star-shaped flower in it. Four cups, also filled with greenery and a single flower, sit in the foreground, while another rests on a stone pillar behind him. In the distance, a guard walks away from the scene down an old cobblestone road.

This is a card of heart-centered giving and sweet connection. That little boy is generously giving a gift to the girl. This is a present from the heart given without strings attached. Think of the way children express love; it is uninhibited by old baggage from the past. They live in the present and express affection without worrying whether their heart is in danger. That white star-shaped flower not only reflects the pure vibration of innocence but also brings that hope and purity down to the earthiness of the five-pointed star of the pentacle. It's hope, dreams, and wishes brought into reality.

This card also evokes a sense of trustworthiness. The watchman that we see walking away from the scene means that all is well, and that we are safe. There is no need to be guarded or overly watchful. The shield with the cross of St. Andrew is a symbol of protection, shielding the children from spiritual danger, and the red hoods that the children are wearing represent protection from physical danger.

This card also directly refers to childhood, either children in the present or our own childhood in the past. In fact, that quality of the past is a strong theme when this card appears, childhood friends or romances from our past may reappear or become more important to us. Sometimes it's about having a connection with someone new who feels like an old friend and with whom we may have had a past life experience, so we are, in essence, reconnecting. This quality may also show up as remembering days gone by and those memories may be influencing our current situation.

The Keys to the Treasure Chest— Key Symbols of the Six of Cups

Boy giving cup to girl—open-hearted generosity, innocent affection, unconditional love

Children—youth, childhood, the past, people from our past, past lives

Cup on the pillar—loving emotion held in high esteem, promises being honored

Four cups on the ground—more love that has yet to be given, gifts keep flowing

Red hoods—protection from earthly danger

Shield with cross—spiritual protection, being shielded from danger

Star-shaped flower—high vibration hopes manifested into reality

Watchman—all is well, you are safe, it is safe to give and receive love

The Wizard's Words of Wisdom— What the Six of Cups Signifies in a Reading

Approach the topic without preconceived notions or prejudice

Give and receive freely with an open heart

Revive your childlike wonder

The best from the past returns to you

Your heart is safe

Behind the Mysterious Door—Journal Questions to Explore the Six of Cups More Deeply

What gift can I give? What gift can I acknowledge receiving?

Magic Words—Affirmation for the Six of Cups

"I love with an open heart."

Your Adventure with the Seven of Cups

Seven of Cups

A figure in silhouette looks on in wonder at a mystical cloud supporting seven golden goblets. In each chalice is a different mystical image: a woman's head, a veiled figure, a snake, a castle, an overflowing pile of jewels, a dragon, and, in a chalice with a skull image on the side, a laurel wreath.

Do you remember the scene in *Indiana Jones and the Last Crusade,* where Indy is faced with dozens of chalices and he has to choose the one that is the true Holy Grail or his father will die? That's what comes to mind when I see this card. We are being faced with making a critical decision— some selections are tempting, others are potentially dangerous. How do we decide which one is the true and best choice?

Fortunately, when this card appears, we are not usually facing life or death decisions, but even those that set our life on a certain course are hard enough to make, and if there are multiple choices, it can be downright confusing. There are other cards that look at choice, the Two of Swords for example, but the Seven of Cups tells us that whatever choice we are making is better made with intuition rather than logic. In other words, choosing with your heart and not your head will lead to the better outcome.

The clouds in this card represent the idea of fantasy, meaning that the choices may or may not exist. Imagining all the possibilities is a great thing as long as it doesn't start to overwhelm us. We've all done that thing where you start looking at all the possible "what-ifs" of a situation, even if they are completely outlandish. When this card shows up, we may want to ask if contemplating all the possible outcomes is inspiring us or are we are creating our own confusion by fantasizing about too many contingencies.

While the main message of this card is about having a variety of choices, the individual symbols in the cups are interesting and, if one jumps out at you in the reading, it may shed some light on the choices that are being considered or that may come up. The cup with the floating head can represent a particular person influencing the choice or our own internal wisdom. The veiled figure stands for keeping secrets, sacred mysteries, or some hidden unknown. The snake can represent rebirth or it can represent a choice that is risky. The castle can be interpreted as protection and stability or long-term goals of personal power. The jewels can stand for wealth and luxury or for using gemstone energies to ground and stabilize us. The laurel wreath in the cup with a skull image symbolizes success and victory. It can also mean victory over death or that success comes with sacrifice. The dragon can either be a powerful and protective ally or forces that need to be vanquished. When we choose with our intuition, one choice will stand out for us like a radiant beam of light.

The Seven of Cups can also indicate that we need to have many choices to compare them and choose the right one. When it comes to love, for example, if we have just one potential lover, we might not know if he is our best option. But if we have many suitors, we can compare them all and one will stand out for us, just as the cup with the veiled figure shines with its glowing red aura.

The Keys to the Treasure Chest—
Key Symbols of the Seven of Cups

Castle —building long-term goals, protection

Cloud—fantasies, imagination, spiritual choices

Cups—making choices intuitively, choosing with your gut

Dragon—powerful protection, challenges

Figure with his back to us—facing choices, being "in the dark"

Head—advice from others or inner wisdom

Jewels—wealth and luxury, working with gemstones magically

Laurel wreath and skull—success, victory over death, gain comes with sacrifice

Snake—an opportunity to recreate yourself, risky endeavors

Veiled figure—hidden mysteries, spiritual truths yet to be revealed

The Wizard's Words of Wisdom—
What the Seven of Cups Signifies in a Reading

Choosing with your heart and not your head

Imagining all the possibilities

Many opportunities presenting themselves

Needing to have multiple choices so that you can pick the best one

Using intuition to guide your decision making

Behind the Mysterious Door—Journal Question
to Explore the Seven of Cups More Deeply

In the choice that I'm facing, what does my heart say?

Magic Words—Affirmation for the Seven of Cups

"I trust my inner guidance to lead me to the right choice."

Your Adventure with the Eight of Cups

Eight of Cups

We see a traveler hiking away from us using a walking staff. A mystical moon is eclipsing the sun and shines over a marsh and a dark, craggy peak in the distance. In the foreground we see eight cups stacked up on the shore.

This man may be beginning a journey, but he'll be back. He's left his cups sitting on the shore, waiting there for his return. Perhaps he'll even return with the missing cup that will complete the top row. When we see this card, we are witnessing someone walking away from something—a job, a relationship, home—but the energy is always one of a temporary break. He is not burning any bridges; this isn't leaving for good. This card is about "recharging your batteries." Some of us need to retreat from demanding situations and revive ourselves. This can be through relaxation, time spent alone, pursuing a hobby, being with friends. It's up to each of us to determine what it is that fills our cup so that we can come back to the things that we love and be fully present. The moon eclipsing the sun echoes that temporarily "hidden" quality. The eclipse means that the sun is going away for a bit but not forever. The sun represents being visible and connected to the energetic experience of life, while the moon represents more of that quality of going within. So, in essence, your inner world is eclipsing your outer world for a time of recharging and rejuvenation. The watery marsh represents making our way through some potentially challenging emotional or spiritual terrain and having the courage to meet those demands, like those large rocks, head on.

One of the main focuses of this card is the lack of permanence and the "coming and going" energy it expresses. If we are looking at a career question, for example, it means it's possible to leave a job behind and look for something that offers a little more challenge or takes us to a higher level. If you do, you aren't burning a bridge with your former employer. You can always go back to the old job, if you wish. If we're looking at a relationship question, this card can mean that one member of the couple may need time on her own to recharge her energy so she can enjoy spending time with her partner when they reunite. If the relationship has broken up, it indicates that the one who left will be coming back. This card can also signify that travel and exploration will help you to find the missing piece of the puzzle that you are facing.

The Keys to the Treasure Chest—
Key Symbols of the Eight of Cups

Eclipse—hiding from sight, retreating temporarily

Eight cups—circumstances that can be made even more fulfilling

Large rocks—making your way around obstacles, meeting challenges head on

Marsh—avoiding potential pitfalls, making your way carefully

Red cloak and boots—pursuing earthly experiences, passion in adventure

Traveler—seeking, taking a break, leaving something while holding space to return

Walking staff—the pursuit of passion and renewed enthusiasm

The Wizard's Words of Wisdom—
What the Eight of Cups Signifies in a Reading

Leaving and then returning

Parting without burning a bridge

Retreating to rejuvenate

Taking risks to discover the missing pieces

Venturing out of your comfort zone

Behind the Mysterious Door—Journal Question to Explore the Eight of Cups More Deeply

What recharges my batteries?

Magic Words—Affirmation for the Eight of Cups

"I can venture out, discover, and come back safely."

Your Adventure with the Nine of Cups

Nine of Cups

A plump and prosperous man sits on a plain wooden bench with his legs splayed and his arms crossed across his chest. His face reflects a sense of contentment and satisfaction. Behind him, a curved banquet table with a blue tablecloth holds nine golden chalices.

We see in this card a man who has it all—the nine cups on the table represent the fulfillment of all his emotional needs. He's content and satisfied. Imagine having nine goblets of wine to drink! That's enough to satisfy your thirst with even some left over to share with others. The fact that these cups are sitting on a banquet table indicates that he's waiting for friends to arrive and share his good fortune. The blue tablecloth indicates that the source of this abundance was acting on his own intuitive inspiration. The white tunic indicates that there is a high spiritual quality to his generosity, but his red turban points to his mind being on the sensual enjoyment of life's pleasures. His arms crossed across his chest are reminiscent of the young man in the Four of Cups. He might be willing to share his bounty, but he may still feel the need to protect his heart and his deepest desires.

When this card appears in a reading, the focus is on satisfaction, getting what you want, feeling emotionally fulfilled. A lovely piece of tarot lore is that this card is called "the wish card," and when it shows up, you can be assured that your wish will be fulfilled. When I turn this card over, I always look at it as the opportunity to make a wish and to see that wish come true.

The Keys to the Treasure Chest—
Key Symbols of the Nine of Cups

Arms across chest—protecting the heart

Blue tablecloth—abundance comes from trusting intuitive inspiration

Red turban—enjoying the sensual pleasures of life

Satisfied man—getting all that you are asking for, feeling satisfied with outcomes

White tunic—connecting to a higher spiritual purpose

The Wizard's Words of Wisdom—
What the Nine of Cups Signifies in a Reading

Emotional fulfillment

Much to be grateful for

Satisfaction with what you already have

Sharing your bounty with others

Your wishes coming true

Behind the Mysterious Door—Journal Question
to Explore the Nine of Cups More Deeply

What do I have in abundance that I can share with others?

Magic Words—Affirmation for the Nine of Cups

"My wishes come true in perfect timing."

Your Adventure with the Ten of Cups

Ten of Cups

A giant rainbow appears in the sky. Within its bands of glowing color float ten golden goblets. A man and woman stand side by side, the man holding the woman close with his arm around her waist. They look up in wonder, each raising an arm to the miraculous rainbow above. Next to them, two little children dance and play with each other while, in the distance, a river flows through some small tree-covered hills toward a little cottage with a red roof.

It's clear that this is a card expressing happiness. Seeing a shimmering arc of color in the sky is joyful and awe-inspiring. Only the most cynical people don't stop and point out a rainbow when it appears. The wonder that we feel is highlighted by the fact that rainbows follow rain. When this card appears in a reading, it indicates that no matter how hard things have been, what will follow, or is following, is a miracle that will bring intense joy.

The happy family on this card also indicates a "domestic" happiness. The kind of contentment we feel in a cozy home life. It may not be an ecstatic frenzy, but more the kind of joy we feel when we take the time to pause and appreciate being around those we love and who love us. If we are not experiencing this in our life now, the river of change will flow and lead us to that happy home in our hearts.

This card can directly indicate the sort of family life or interactions with others that have that snuggly closeness—one where the partners are completely content with their commitment and the children (or the projects that are their "children") are joyful and bring joy. It is worth noting too that the children are so happy with each other that they take the rainbow for granted. The blessings that come down are so plentiful that we can focus on those around us.

The Keys to the Treasure Chest—
Key Symbols of the Ten of Cups

Arms upraised—noticing and appreciating the blessings received

Close couple—love, commitment, joyful marriage, cozy family-like partnerships

Dancing children—playfulness, joy, taking blessings as a given

Hills—life is effortless and the small bumps are easy to handle

House —tranquil home life, moving in together, establishing a cozy partnership

Rainbow—joy, happiness, synchronicities, blessings

Red and blue clothing—accessing intuition and enjoying sensual pleasures

River—flowing toward happiness, change brings joy

Ten cups—total emotional fulfillment

Trees—growth and protection around your happiness

The Wizard's Words of Wisdom—
What the Ten of Cups Signifies in a Reading

Happiness and peaceful contentment

Home and hearth

The end of difficulties and arrival of joyful relief

Taking time to notice the love around us

Warm cozy feelings in the heart

Behind the Mysterious Door—Journal Question
to Explore the Ten of Cups More Deeply

What miracle would I like to manifest?

Magic Words—Affirmation for the Ten of Cups

"I radiate love and peaceful happiness everywhere I go."

[10]

The Grounded Earthiness of the Pentacles

Finally, we come to the reliable stability of the Pentacles. Pentacles represent the element of earth—strong, long lasting, secure, solid, slow, and steady. Think of the things that we associate with earth: rocks, mountains, soil, metals. In the cycle of manifestation, Pentacles represent the end result. After we've come up with the idea (air), acted on that idea (fire), given it soul and magic (water), we end up with the final manifestation, usually something material, and that's what earth and Pentacles represent.

Pentacles are gold discs, reminiscent of gold coins, which can often refer to issues regarding money, financial stability, jobs, or other means of income. They also have another meaning. That five-pointed star represents the human body with a head and arms and legs outstretched. So, Pentacles also represent physical issues of the body and its health. However, that star is also something even more magical. Beyond being just a physical body, we are made up of stardust. Pentacles symbolize the tangible, practical world around us, and the spirit that has brought that manifestation into being. It's important to see that spirit through the material.

It's interesting to note that the word "pentacle" itself can mean an amulet, any amulet, not just one with a five-pointed star. Amulets are magical items, usually something worn, with the power to protect the wearer and are often are made of metal. In many older versions of the tarot, this was the suit of Coins, but in the RWS, the suit is translated into something more magical than a mere coin. Certainly, coins mean material security, but a gold amulet means material security with an added spiritual element.

When we see Pentacles, it's good to think of the qualities of earth. Mountains don't move—it takes eons to change their shape and structure. So issues with the Pentacles are slow-moving and long lasting. Like mountains, they conjure up ideas of might and strength but they also bring to mind the fertile qualities of the rich soil that gives plants a place to feed and stabilize their roots. Pentacles also symbolize the shiny allure of gems and precious metals and the protectiveness of the stone walls of a fortress. So, when you see Pentacles show up in your reading, tap into these possibilities and see how they relate to the question at hand.

Your Adventure with the Ace of Pentacles

Ace of Pentacles

We are standing in a flowering garden. Lilies grow among the grasses and a hedge of roses opens up into an arched gateway. A sandy path runs beneath the arch toward snowy mountains in the distance. A glowing hand holding a large golden disc emerges from a cloud. On the disc is the image of a five-pointed star.

As with all of the Aces, you are being given a gift. With the Ace of Pentacles, a divine hand is giving you something material. It may be money, it may be a new job, it may be improved health. Whatever it is, it represents the pure essence of earth energy—safe, secure, solid. When this card appears in your reading, the question to ask yourself is "what will make me feel rooted and grounded?" and that is what you are beginning to manifest.

The hand holding the pentacle is hovering over an enclosed garden, a symbol not only of the safety of that barrier and the serenity and calm that a garden offers, but also the beautiful abundance of the flowers that grow there. The lilies represent spiritual abundance while the roses represent an abundance of earthly enjoyment. That archway symbolizes the gateway between the garden and the outside world. You have a choice. You can stay in the safety of the garden or you can take what you gained in the garden with you to climb the mountains ahead to higher levels of enlightenment.

Like all paths in the tarot, the pathway here indicates a journey—moving ahead toward growth and success. To get to your next step, you must pass through the arch, which symbolizes transition from one state to another. Once you leave the garden, you become someone else and cannot return to the being you were before. You are initiated into new mysteries and "grow up," in a sense, into an expanded version of yourself. Take that initiation seriously and welcome the growth.

The Keys to the Treasure Chest—
Key Symbols of the Ace of Pentacles

Archway—gateways to new ways of being, knowledge, initiation

Cloud—something coming from nothing

Garden—sensual pleasures, being divinely protected, growth, abundance

Hand—divine offerings, being given a material gift

Lilies—high vibration spiritual gifts, the spirit behind the material gift

Mountains—future challenges that bring reward

Path—a journey, movement initiated by you, choosing your trail

Pentacle—a new job, new abundance, a new version of health, a "Yes" from Spirit

Red roses—enjoyment of the senses, material pleasure

The Wizard's Words of Wisdom—
What the Ace of Pentacles Signifies in a Reading

A "Yes" from the Universe

Financial gain being handed to you

Improved health

New opportunities for manifestation

The pure essence of stability and security

Behind the Mysterious Door—Journal Question to Explore the Ace of Pentacles More Deeply

What can I manifest to bring more security?

Magic Words—Affirmation for the Ace of Pentacles

"I am able to manifest all that I desire."

Your Adventure with the Two of Pentacles

Two of Pentacles

We enter into a scene with a young juggler dressed in fanciful clothes. He is wearing a comically tall red cap and a brown leather jerkin that was, at one time, decoratively cut along the bottom, but now appears to be tattered. He holds a pentacle in each hand. They are connected by a green ribbon in the shape of a *lemniscate*, or an infinity symbol. In the background, two small ships sail over a sea that rocks with roller coaster–like waves.

We've all heard the word "juggling" used to describe a situation where we have taken on more than what we usually can handle. There are times when juggling is inevitable or necessary, and that's what this card represents. Because this card deals with the material world, we can interpret it directly as taking money from one part of your life and feeding it to another, such as pawning your jewelry to get money to pay the rent. This card can also mean having more than one job, a job and a side business, or even a dream that could become a side business someday. It can also indicate juggling health issues. You may be dealing with an illness and while the medicine you are taking helps with the sickness, it has some side effects that are not pleasant. Or it may mean sacrificing your sleep to get up early to go running. The card can also be about more than just juggling health and money. With the way that his hat is shaped, it can even sometimes mean juggling more than one relationship! When this image appears, it's definitely an indicator that you can do the juggling, at least for a while. But, eventually it will get to be a roller coaster ride like those boats in the background are experiencing, and it takes a lot of effort to keep from dropping those discs.

Fortunately, you have a little extra divine help keeping it all together in the form of that infinity symbol. Have fun with the experience. Some things may fall apart, such as the hem of your clothing, but that doesn't mean you can't show off your multitasking skill. It's quite possible to enjoy the experience on the material level, all the red that he's wearing indicates that there's pleasure to be had in handling everything and doing it well. You're surefooted in those green shoes, which represent growth. Material gain is possible from taking on more than one project and you have the sense of balance and grace to do it.

The Keys to the Treasure Chest—
Key Symbols of the Two of Pentacles

Juggler—ability to handle more than one project or goal simultaneously

Lemniscate—connection to the infinite divine, you are being spiritually supported

Red hat, belt, and leggings—moving easily in the world of sensual pleasure

Ships—trade and commerce, travel, managing the ups and downs

Two pentacles—split focus, doubling your success by diversifying

Waves—riding out the climbs and dips

The Wizard's Words of Wisdom—
What the Two of Pentacles Signifies in a Reading

Having fun with your juggling act

Material gain from taking on more than one project

Robbing Peter to pay Paul

Spiritually supported multitasking

Wearing multiple hats

Behind the Mysterious Door—Journal Question to Explore the Two of Pentacles More Deeply

What extra project have I always wanted to take on?

Magic Words—Affirmation for the Two of Pentacles

"I handle multiple tasks with grace and ease."

Your Adventure with the Three of Pentacles

Three of Pentacles

We step into a church and see three men discussing a carved stone archway that is being built. A stonemason, dressed in an apron, stands on a bench with an old-fashioned mallet in his hand looking as if he has just paused what he is doing to have a discussion with the other two. An architect, wearing a medieval cowl, is holding the plans, while the monk with his dark robes and shaved head, is looking on. Above them, we see the delicately and expertly carved arch with three pentacles in a triangle pointing upward, while below that, a triangle pointing downward holds the image of a stylized five petaled rose.

The Three of Pentacles is about teamwork. We see three people here: a craftsman, a designer, and a patron. Each needs the others to get the job done. Without the architect, no one would know what to build; without the mason, there would be no stonework; and without the monk providing the money, neither of the other two could be hired. Like a stool with three legs, each needs the other two for the whole thing to stand. If one is missing, the whole project falls apart.

Since I have a tarot reading salon in Los Angeles, I see many clients from the film industry and this card will often appear in questions of work. It perfectly expresses what happens in moviemaking. Many people come together, each with their specialized skills—producers, writers, directors, actors, costumers, and so on—to make a finished product that will make them all money. There is a lovely "well-oiled machine" quality about the Three of Pentacles. They are all talented, know what their roles are, and work together in unison to make something beautiful in the material world.

The three pentacles pointing in an upward triangle represents the element of fire, or action and motion. This is not a static Pentacle card but one showing the action of the creation of material things. The downward triangle below represents the alchemical element of water bringing Spirit to the project. The symbolic rose has an interesting history. In ancient times up through the Middle Ages, five petaled roses were carved into decorations to indicate that what was said there was kept secret or *sub rosa*—under the rose. It was the medieval version of "what happens in Vegas, stays in Vegas." So, this plan may have elements that are on a "need to know" basis.

When this card shows up in a reading, it means that harmonious connections and working with others are highlighted. It can mean on the job, of course, but it could mean working with others on another kind of purposeful project; for example, volunteering for something meaningful to you, organizing as a committee, or taking a class. Look for ways in which working alongside other like-minded souls will expand your dreams and opportunities.

The Keys to the Treasure Chest— Key Symbols of the Three of Pentacles

Apron—Masonic symbol of innocence and honor

Architect—the one who conceives of the ideas

Column—the strength upholding the project

Downward triangle—soul, harmony, cooperation

Mallet—Masonic symbol of authority and control

Monk—the one who provides the materials to bring the vision into reality

Rose—*sub rosa*, keeping certain elements within the group only

Stonemason—the one who brings the vision into reality through action

Three pentacles—manifesting something both beautiful and prosperous

Upward triangle—action, creativity, energy

The Wizard's Words of Wisdom—
What the Three of Pentacles Signifies in a Reading

Allying with other experts to create something beautiful

Gathering together with like-minded people

Keeping your project under wraps for now

Manifesting your dreams and desires with the help of others

Working harmoniously alongside others

Behind the Mysterious Door—Journal Question
to Explore the Three of Pentacles More Deeply

Who is on my team and what meaningful things are we
creating?

Magic Words—Affirmation for the Three of Pentacles

"Together we can create anything."

Your Adventure with the Four of Pentacles

Four of Pentacles

A king dressed in a simple tunic sits alone on a small stone bench far outside a walled city. He has a rather plain crown on his head adorned only with a large gold pentacle disc. He holds another pentacle in his arms and steps on two more, holding them down with his feet.

If we look at the Pentacles as being coins, it's easy to discern what's going on here. We have a man who is holding on very tightly to his money. Normally, it might make sense to keep an eye on your material possessions, but here we have someone who is sitting outside of town with nobody around to bother him. We don't see any robbers; we don't see any pickpockets. This guy is alone. And *still* he hangs on to his coins like his life depends on it. That's what we might call paranoid or, at least, overly protective. There's nothing for him to worry about, he can relax, but still he's on guard waiting for something bad to happen. This card shows up around situations where we are worried that the worst is going to happen but we have no evidence that it will. So when it appears, it can be a sign that your negative thinking is creating unnecessary worry.

Those pentacles are truly getting in the way of the King's enjoyment. He's wearing a crown, which is generally a symbol for being connected with divine energy, but in his case, there is a pentacle between his crown and the heavens. He's being so protective, has his material possessions so much on his mind, that his access to divine energy through the crown chakra is blocked. He's also placed that protective shield over his heart. He's closed off entirely. I sometimes get the image of a tortoise who has pulled his head and legs into his shell. He's hunkered down. If you're actually being threatened, this kind of behavior can be appropriate, but if there is no risk around, then it's being too anxious.

Compared to the other kings in the tarot, this one is dressed rather plainly. Even some of the regular people in the tarot are dressed more fabulously than he is. This guy has wealth but he's not showing it off. Is that modesty or being miserly?

Numerologically, the number four has the essence of stability, so when we mix that in with the stability of the element of earth, it's a little bit of overkill. Things are stuck, immobile, and fossilized. The way he is clinging to his material possessions has a quality of being overly possessive and that can apply to more than just things—it can mean overly controlling with relationships, too.

When the Four of Pentacles appears, sometimes it's a message that you need to hunker down and hide out for a while, but more often it's about awakening to the idea that, while being safe may be necessary sometimes, being shut off, possessive, and worried about nonexistent threats may be blocking us from receiving our blessings, too.

The Keys to the Treasure Chest— Key Symbols of the Four of Pentacles

City in the distance—isolation, you are safe from danger

Four pentacles—stagnant, stuck energy, rigidity

Pentacle on crown—blocking our connection to the divine

Pentacle over chest—blocking connection to emotions, holding onto what's mine

Pentacles under feet—immobility, not able to take a step forward

Plain clothing—modesty or miserliness, lack of enjoyment

Stone bench—self-denial, stubbornness

The Wizard's Words of Wisdom—
What the Four of Pentacles Signifies in a Reading

>Fear is blocking you from your spiritual connection

>If you are being threatened, creating a safe space will help

>Jealousy can be replaced with openness

>Worry is unnecessary

>You are safe

Behind the Mysterious Door—Journal Question
to Explore the Four of Pentacles More Deeply

>What unnecessary worries am I ready to release?

Magic Words—Affirmation for the Four of Pentacles

>"I replace fear with love."

Your Adventure with the Five of Pentacles

Five of Pentacles

It's a snowy night. We see two poor people dressed in tattered clothes outside of a church. The woman is walking barefoot through the snow, while the man is walking with crutches. He has rags on his feet and a bell around his neck. Above them, light shines through a stained-glass window made up of five pentacles arranged in the shape of a plant. Surrounding the golden discs are abundant leaves and red roses with two towers at the top.

I call this card the "pity party." You know, we've all been to that place where we look at our situation cynically and say out loud to anyone who will listen, "Why me?" When we first look at this card, we may be tempted to see the poor people shivering in the cold and think "poor them," too! But taking a closer look, we see that there is more to the story. The stained-glass window has light shining through it. That means that the church is open. All they have to do is go inside and they can at least get out of the snow and get warm. And a church with a loving and giving congregation would even be able to feed them and find them some clothing and shelter.

Have you ever known someone who was so entrenched in wallowing in their misery that you began to think that they actually enjoyed it? Complaining can sometimes feel cathartic but, like a drug, if you keep at it, it can get to be an addiction. Sometimes there can even be a pride in the suffering—a "look at all I am going through" quality that a person can wear like a badge of honor. The folks in this card are out in the cold and yet they could be inside if they would take the initiative to find the door.

It's not as if they don't have issues. They do. They're dressed in rags, they're out in the snow, and the bell around the man's neck was a medieval symbol of someone with leprosy. There is definitely some heavy stuff going down. But the window gives a clue as to other possibilities for them. The green leaves and the plant with the pentacle blossoms indicate that growth, health, and prosperity are available to them. The roses say they could experience some pleasure. And the towers that appear at the top, they are almost unnoticeable, but they are important. Every time we see two towers, they represent a gateway we can walk through into an expanded version of ourselves. This couple is being offered an alternate reality—one of health, wealth, and evolution. They may have to find their way to it, but it is most certainly there and available to them.

So, when this card shows up in a reading, ask yourself: "How are my beliefs preventing me from seeing other, better possibilities?" "Where am I stuck in the pity party?" and "How can I get out of my current state into an improved situation?" Watch the stories that you are telling yourself. Are you saying things like "I'll never get out of debt" or "bragging" about how much money you racked up in student loans or having a verbal competition with others about who has the worst health? Be careful with those kinds of "spells" as they may be keeping you out in the cold instead of letting you into the warm church filled with kind people willing to help.

The Keys to the Treasure Chest— Key Symbols of the Five of Pentacles

> Bell—communicating lack, keeping good fortune away
>
> Crutches—unhealthy reliance on others, using addictions as a crutch
>
> Green leaves—vitality, change, new beginnings are available
>
> People dressed in tatters—feelings of lack, self-pity, pride in suffering
>
> Plant with pentacles—growth of health and wealth
>
> Roses—renewed enjoyment in earthly pleasures
>
> Snow—being "frozen" or stuck in negative thinking

Stained-glass window—warmth, shelter, light, divine blessing within reach

Two towers—opportunity to transform and leave the suffering behind

The Wizard's Words of Wisdom—
What the Five of Pentacles Signifies in a Reading

Being able to attain stability again

Feeling shut out

Feeling victimized

Focusing on lack and poverty

Having the opportunity to transform your destiny

Behind the Mysterious Door—Journal Question
to Explore the Five of Pentacles More Deeply

How can I transform my feelings of victimization into belief in myself?

Magic Words—Affirmation for the Five of Pentacles

"I have access to feelings of confidence and empowerment."

Your Adventure with the Six of Pentacles

Six of Pentacles

Outside of a town, we see a wealthy merchant standing next to two beggars in patched clothing who are holding their hands out asking for money. The merchant is holding an old-fashioned balance scale with one hand and with the other he is dropping four coins into one man's hands while three coins remain in his palm. The other man is holding his hands out, still waiting to receive.

This is a card about our relationship to the concept of "flow." The wealthy merchant is redistributing his wealth to two poor beggars. Six pentacles float over the scene like a protective roof over the heads of the three men. The merchant has been fortunate enough to make a living and have some to spare, so he is sharing it with those less fortunate than he is to bring the balance we see represented in that scale he's holding. He will have less and the poor people will have more and all will be well. He is dropping four coins into the hands of one of the poor men, four being the number of stability in numerology. Three coins remain in his hand, which is the number for expansion. Either he will give this energy of growth to the other poor man or he will keep this money and expand his abundance so that he can give more. The coins total seven, which is the number representing blessings.

The three men in this image (there's that number three again) are dressed in different colors. The man dressed in tan with the bandage on his head is concerned with survival. The bandage represents that a physical injury or mental illness is preventing him from being able to meet his basic needs. The man dressed in blue has chosen poverty as a spiritual path; light blue is the color of a sacred connection. He has a red yod emerging from his pocket or patch, representing the blessings that he receives for following this path. The merchant is dressed in a rich red cloak, leggings, sash, and hat, a sign of his enjoyment of worldly pleasure, but his tunic is white and blue, indicating that he is concerned with spiritual matters as well.

When a question about finances comes up, this card asks us to examine our relationship to money. Do we need to give more or are we in a position to receive? To understand this card, you have to first understand what money means. Money itself is a symbol. Those pieces of paper or numbers on your bank statement don't have any intrinsic value. We all make the agreement that the piece of paper that says "one dollar" on it is worth the equivalent of an apple and the same sized paper with "one hundred dollars" on it is the equivalent of dinner for a family at a decent restaurant. When we get paid or pay someone else we are not really exchanging those pieces of paper, we are exchanging energy. When you work, you put your energy, time, and experience into the job and your employer or customer gives you a piece of paper with a number on it. When you purchase that latte at your favorite coffee shop, you give the cashier a piece of paper in exchange for the ingredients, labor, and the other expenses of the business. That piece of paper that you hand over is representative of the energy that you put in at your job. So, when we view it this way, we are simply exchanging energy whenever we gain or spend money. Like a system of pipes, we receive and then we give and the energy flows through us.

Where I find that most people get hung up is that they stop seeing this exchange as a flow of energy and start to give their negative attention to the paper with the numbers on it. "I'm not making enough money," "This costs too much," or "My bills are crushing me!" These kinds of thoughts and statements will block the flow of abundance as surely as a concrete barricade. When someone is in this stuck place, the Six of Pentacles will often appear to remind him to open up that flow.

So, how do we open the flow of our financial plumbing? One of the best ways we can do that is by calling in the spiritual plumber called "Gratitude" to snake our drain. By being appreciative of our exchanges, both receiving and giving, we can open up and allow more to flow through us. When you receive your paycheck, take a moment to appreciate receiving this money. When you pay a bill, instead of complaining about the money going out of your bank account, say a word of appreciation for what you received in exchange for that money.

This card may be directly about the flow of money, but it can also represent other kinds of flow as well. Are we balanced in giving and receiving emotionally or are we being too much of a giver or a taker? Are we expressing our gratitude for the divine blessings that we receive or are we feeling entitled? Are we using our talents to share with the world or are we hoarding those gifts out of fear? When this card appears in a reading, look for ways to open up more flow in all areas of your life.

The Keys to the Treasure Chest— Key Symbols of the Six of Pentacles

Bandage—injury, mental illness

Blue and white clothing—spiritual connection

Castle—safety, structure, abundance

Merchant—wealth, worldly concerns, mastery over the material world

Poor men—feelings of not enough, self-denial

Red clothing—connection to earthly pleasures

Scale—balanced flow, harmony, redistribution, recalibrating for equality

Tan clothing—concerns about basic survival

Trees—growth, expansion, stability

Yod—divine blessings

The Wizard's Words of Wisdom— What the Six of Pentacles Signifies in a Reading

Balancing your give and take

Energy flowing between you and others

Gratitude for money going out and money coming in

Prosperity wanting to flow to you

Using material wealth as a blessing to yourself and others

Behind the Mysterious Door—Journal Question to Explore the Six of Pentacles More Deeply

Where is my flow blocked and how can I use gratitude to open it up?

Magic Words—Affirmation for the Six of Pentacles

"Energy and prosperity flow easily through me."

Your Adventure with the Seven of Pentacles

Seven of Pentacles

We see a gardener standing in his garden leaning on his hoe. He's looking over at a bush that he has carefully raised from a seed into the lush productive plant that is bearing fruit in the form of shiny golden pentacles.

Have you ever experienced growing a plant from a seed? There is something so satisfying about gardening. We prepare the soil, remove the rocks and weeds, fertilize, make little rows, plant our seeds, and cover them with the rich earth. Then we water and wait, and water and wait some more. Finally, after what seems like forever, we see little sprouts poke up out of the ground. We cover these seedlings with protective plastic, build little fences around them, wrap tendrils around climbing frames and trellises, and yank out the weeds and pull off the pests. Finally, our little plants grow up into hardy bushes and begin flowering and then, after some sexy pollination magic (thank you, bees and butterflies), fruits and vegetables begin to grow. Then, one magical day, they are ripe. We have a harvest. We can feed ourselves, our families, and, if we're really good gardeners, our friends and neighbors with the bounty.

In this card's image, we are catching the gardener at the moment that he is thoughtfully looking at his abundant crop. He's resting after all the tending and care that he has given to his garden and reflecting on his success. When we see this card show up in a reading, it's a time for us to reflect on where we are in the cycle of growth. Are we looking at the end of the cycle where we are admiring the fruits of our labor? Are we in the middle of tending to something that will eventually pay off? Or are we just now planting the seeds of the amazing things to come?

Regardless of where we are in the cycle, this card indicates that time and energy will have to be devoted to the venture and not to expect instant results. Remember all that waiting for the seed to even sprout? This is a card of investment, either a financial investment that will pay off or investing our time, energy, and heart into something that will reward us with even more than we put in.

A very small but powerful symbol in this card is found in the tiny, curly tendrils that extend from the plant. Plants create tendrils to attach to a support of some kind so that they can grow higher. Think of the support that you need to make your project a success, whether it's financial, emotional, or in the form of an extra pair of hands.

The Keys to the Treasure Chest—
Key Symbols of the Seven of Pentacles

> Blue leggings and shirt—mystical, intuitive, and emotionally invested
>
> Brown boots—feet firmly planted on the ground
>
> Bush with pentacles—fruits of our labor, results, rewards
>
> Gardener—actively tending to our projects
>
> Golden orange tunic—opening the way for new ventures
>
> Green leaves—growth, vitality
>
> Hoe—labor, weeding out distractions
>
> Mountains—overcoming challenges in the distance
>
> Tendrils—reaching out for support

The Wizard's Words of Wisdom—
What the Seven of Pentacles Signifies in a Reading

> Actively seeking support
>
> Growing and expanding
>
> Planting seeds that will pay off later
>
> Stepping back to admire your handiwork
>
> Tending to your venture

Behind the Mysterious Door—Journal Questions to Explore the Seven of Pentacles More Deeply

What seeds have I planted? How am I tending to those seeds?

Magic Words—Affirmation for the Seven of Pentacles

"Anything I touch magically grows."

Your Adventure with the Eight of Pentacles

Eight of Pentacles

We are in an outdoor workshop where a craftsman is hammering stars into golden pentacle discs with a chisel. So that's where all these pentacles are coming from! He's focused on the task and has displayed six of his discs on the wooden panel in front of him. One of the discs has been set off to the side under the bench.

This card is about "practice makes perfect" and skill leading to abundance. Musicians have to practice scales to become fluid players or singers. Artists have to make thousands of drawings and paintings before becoming masters. Medical residents have to treat hundreds of patients while being supervised before they can become doctors.

It's this kind of work that leads to success.

The craftsman in this card has been working at this for a while, and as a result has built a collection of discs on the wall—or since that wall is made of wood, we could say that he's using his skill to build his own money tree. But unlike the gardener in the Seven of Pentacles who has accomplished his goal and is taking a rest, he's continuing to work on getting better and better.

This card reflects the sometimes repetitive nature of building something solid, strong, and long lasting. If we are going to build up a savings account, a little amount invested bit by bit adds up. If we want to get a good job, we have to work at getting good grades on tests to get into college. If we are going to build a business of our own, we have to take care of all the potentially boring details like getting a business license, printing business cards, and building a website. If this card shows up in a reading about relationships, it's an indication that you will have to work at something consistently to see the positive result of stability and growth—going out on dates, changing your habits, or even going to couples therapy.

The craftsman has put his best work up on the wall to display, but you'll notice that there's one disc that has been set off to the side because it wasn't good enough to show others. This is a reminder that making mistakes is part of the process of becoming skilled. Set those mistakes aside, learn from them, and continue to work at your project.

The Keys to the Treasure Chest—
Key Symbols of the Eight of Pentacles

Black apron—protection, willingness to get your hands dirty

Blue shirt—using intuition

Craftsman—skill building, talent and practice equal success, working at something

Hammer, chisel, and block—having the necessary tools for success

Pentacle on the bench—continuing to work toward your goal

Pentacle under the bench—making mistakes is part of the process

Pentacles on the wall—building abundance and success through practice

Red leggings and shoes—finding pleasure in the work

Road—an open path to get to your goal, your plans will work

Walled city—accessing success when others do not

Workbench—support for your goals

The Wizard's Words of Wisdom—
What the Eight of Pentacles Signifies in a Reading

Building your money tree

Crafting prosperity through labor

Perfecting your skills

Recognizing that failure is part of the learning process

Working consistently on your project

Behind the Mysterious Door—Journal Question to Explore the Eight of Pentacles More Deeply

What are the next three steps of my plan?

Magic Words—Affirmation for the Eight of Pentacles

"Practicing makes me a master."

Your Adventure with the Nine of Pentacles

Nine of Pentacles

We see an elegantly dressed noblewoman in a vineyard. A hooded falcon perches on a gloved hand while her other hand rests on one of the nine pentacles nestled among the lush grapevines behind her. A little snail crawls on the sandy path in front of her.

The woman in the Nine of Pentacles is enjoying life to the fullest. Instead of seeing someone who is toiling over a project, we see someone who is partaking of enjoyable pursuits—training falcons and winemaking. I call her "the lady of leisure." She's not someone who takes her good fortune for granted, she uses her time and energy to pursue her passions. When we see this card in a reading, it means paying attention and enjoying the good in our own lives. The woman is standing in front of grapevines that are growing pentacles. Of course, the lush grapevine, heavy with grapes and pentacles ready to be harvested, represents abundance and more pleasures to come. The arrangement of the pentacles is significant too. There are six on her right and three on her left. In numerology, the number six represents harmony and three represents growth, while together, the number nine signifies the attainment of goals. She's reached the top. The prosperity and abundance of the nine pentacles follow the pursuit of her passions. This card holds in it the advice to "do what you love and the money will follow," but there is definitely some discipline involved. You don't get to be a master falconer or winemaker by dabbling. The hooded falcon on her hand attests to that. In ancient times, falcons were used for hunting. Falconers would train wild and dangerous birds to follow their instructions to catch small game. The training of a wild animal requires patience and persistence. Falcons are birds with excellent vision and if they are visually startled, they can cause a lot of damage with their razor sharp claws. Putting that hood over the falcon's eyes calms the bird and allows the trainer to safely control her. The falcon can represent our own wild "hunter" nature—competitive and even bloodthirsty. This woman has reached success by controlling those destructive impulses and keeping her focus on only the goals that bring her joy.

The snail at her feet echoes the quality of earth—slow, steady discipline leads to the result. The snail also travels with his home on his back, representing the woman's self-sufficiency. Her gold-colored gown represents the aura of success around her. The red flower pattern on the gown resembles the symbol of Venus, goddess of love, beauty, and pleasure. Her red cap also connects her to the divine nature of worldly delights. While the mountains in the distance represent the fact that any challenges are a long way off, the two trees represent a sort of natural gateway. Since nine is the number of attainment, it indicates that she has the option of making her way through this gate from the luxury of the vineyard to other new ambitions and challenges.

When this card shows up in a reading, it's a reminder of your own self-sufficiency and a signal to enjoy the life that you have created for yourself. This card can often show up as a message about our "right livelihood," meaning having a career that is both economically and spiritually fulfilling. If you aren't at a place where life is enjoyable, then it's time to take stock of the things that *are* pleasurable in your life and make plans to change the things that are not to your liking.

The Keys to the Treasure Chest—
Key Symbols of the Nine of Pentacles

Chateau—achievement of material goals

Flowers on gown—connection to Venus's attributes: beauty, pleasure, love

Golden gown—success, luxury

Grapevines—abundance, pleasures

Hooded falcon—controlling competitive animal nature

Mountains—challenges are far from the present

Nine pentacles—fulfillment, attainment of goals

Noblewoman—lady of leisure, pleasure in her pursuits

Red cap—divine connection through sensual enjoyment

Snail—self-sufficiency, slow and steady progress achieves the goal

Two trees—gateway to new exciting adventures

The Wizard's Words of Wisdom—
What the Nine of Pentacles Signifies in a Reading

Abundance increases

Do what you love and the money will follow

Enjoy the happiness and pleasures in life

Pursue right livelihood

Self-control brings opportunities for positive indulgence

Behind the Mysterious Door—Journal Question
to Explore the Nine of Pentacles More Deeply

What action can I commit to, to bring more pleasure into my life?

Magic Words—Affirmation for the Nine of Pentacles

"I enjoy so many activities in my life."

Your Adventure with the Ten of Pentacles

Ten of Pentacles

We enter into the courtyard of a villa where members of an extended family are enjoying each other's company under a large archway. An old man is sitting with dogs at his feet while a man and a woman have a conversation. A little child is clinging to the woman's gown and petting one of the dogs. Ten pentacles float mysteriously in the foreground.

This is the only card in the tarot that shows a multigenerational family—child, parent, and grandparent. This is significant. Think about the meaning of the suit of Pentacles: solid, stable, long lasting. This card reflects the stability of lineage, things being handed down from generation to generation. Of course, this can mean things like inheritance and money, but it can also mean the inheritance of physical or personality traits or wisdom being given. It also means that extended family members are involved in the situation at hand. This goes beyond just your immediate family, it can also mean ancestors who have passed on are offering blessings for your venture or can be petitioned for help with your cause.

This concept of lineage also indicates longevity and long-term stability. Whatever you're working on will be lasting—whether it's a business, a marriage, an education, or something else. This idea of family extends beyond our natural family. There is a community feeling in this card. This is not a card of individualism. It is about close and committed connections to others. We're all in this together and together we can create something amazing.

This card also shows the true meaning of prosperity. There is a secret message encoded in this card. The ten pentacles floating in the foreground are arranged in the pattern of the *Ten Sephirot* or the Tree of Life from the Kabbalah. The Tree of Life diagrams how divine energy becomes matter—or how we bring heaven down to earth. The material world is a blessing, abundance is a divine gift, and when we appreciate these spiritual gifts in the material world, we are connecting to the divine. The fact that the old man, who represents wisdom, is also wearing a cloak that is covered with both grapes and esoteric sigils reinforces the understanding of that spirit world/material world connection.

The family members are standing under an archway. They have walked through one of those magical gateways into their abundant and blessed life. You too have arrived there. It's time to take stock of all that you have and all there is to appreciate in order to keep that flow coming to you. On that arch, above the old man's head, we see banners. One depicts balanced scales, a sign that you are getting the blessings you have earned. The amount of conscious gratitude that you put into life equals the blessings that you get out of it. Above the scales, we see a banner with a castle, meaning that we are achieving, building something that will last—a sanctuary for ourselves and our loved ones. The man holding a spear underlines that protective sanctuary message.

There are also some interesting subtle and undefined images. At the left edge, we see a small piece of a mysterious tapestry on the wall. The tapestry depicts a castle on a cliff with a blue wavy sea slowly wearing away at that bluff. This is the flipside to the castle that we see on the banner above. Even the strongest castle will eventually be worn away by the elements. But above that cliffside castle, we see a face with a heart below it (right next to the topmost left pentacle). This reminds us that while the material project is bound to decay, the spirit of what you have created lives on and will be born again in some new form. The black-and-white checkerboard border is that reminder of duality—that light can't exist without dark and that the cycle of life, death, and rebirth is continuous.

The Keys to the Treasure Chest—
Key Symbols of the Ten of Pentacles

Archway—having crossed the point of initiation

Castle and spirit on tapestry—the material will eventually fade but the spirit of the material will live on

Castle banner—sanctuary, success

Child—carrying on the legacy, new fresh energy added onto the project, naiveté

Dogs—loyalty, protection

Man with spear—protection, safety, security

Old man—longevity, ancestors, wisdom

Scales banner—balance, karma

Ten pentacles—Tree of Life, connection of heaven and earth, spiritual manifesting into the material

Woman—nurturing, sensuality

The Wizard's Words of Wisdom—
What the Ten of Pentacles Signifies in a Reading

Connection to ancestors

Long-lasting material blessings

Long-term commitments

Longevity for life, relationships, and projects

The connection of the spiritual to the material

Behind the Mysterious Door—Journal Questions
to Explore the Ten of Pentacles More Deeply

What have I committed to? How can I feed this commitment?

Magic Words—Affirmation for the Ten of Pentacles

"Blessings stay with me forever."

[11]

An Audience with the Court Cards

The court cards are a special grouping of cards that have a different energy than the pip cards. Even though they are grouped up with the pips in the Minor Arcana, these cards have their own vibration.

Like the pips, the court cards fall under the four suits of Swords, Wands, Cups, and Pentacles. Within each of these suits, four characters emerge—the Page, Knight, Queen, and King. In older texts defining these cards, you might see something along the lines of "the Queen of Cups represents a woman over eighteen who has blonde or light colored hair and blue eyes." I find these old descriptions too restrictive. There are three male choices for every suit while there is only one female. There is also a lack of the beautiful racial variety that exists in the world. While the RWS is a rich and gorgeous deck in many ways, my one complaint is this lack of realistic diversity. However, I do realize that it's a product of its time and place and, as a result, I don't take those old-timey descriptions too seriously.

Instead, it's much more useful to look at the general energy that each card's person exudes. The Kings represent the best aspects of the father archetype: authority, top-down leadership, being a provider, maturity, confidence, and the yang/active principle. The Queens represent the mother archetype: partnership, connectedness, influence, shared leadership, facilitating, caretaking, and the yin/receptive principle. The Knights represent the young adult energy: courage, will, ambition, initiation, energy, focus. And, finally, our little Pages. Pages were the messenger boys in the noble court and represent that teenage energy: youth, freshness, enthusiasm, inexperience, beginner-ness, naiveté, and because they're the messengers, they also represent communication.

While in the descriptions, I refer to the Kings, Knights, and Pages as "he" and the Queens as "she," don't get thrown by the apparent genders. A biological woman can just as easily express that "masculine" king energy as a biological man. Likewise, don't get too caught up in the chronological age represented by the court cards. We've all known children who were old souls or fifty-year-olds who act like teenagers. So again, focus on the energies that these cards represent rather than any preconceived notions based on the looks of their characters.

The quickest way to get to the meaning of each card is to combine the energies of the roles with the energies of the suit. If you do that, you can get a general gist of what the card means. So, Page (young, enthusiastic, naive) plus Cups (emotions, love, intuition, spirituality) equals the energy of fresh love, enthusiastic spirituality, and psychic empathy, but perhaps not the most emotionally stable and reliable.

Traditionally, the court cards represented people—this is where the old trope "you will meet a tall, dark stranger" comes from—and depending on the question and the layout, these cards *can* indicate a person around the questioner. But, I find that just as often they represent something within the questioner herself. This is something that just comes up for most readers intuitively, but there are definitely layouts where certain positions can indicate the questioner, other positions can indicate other people, while still other positions can represent qualities outside of the individuals involved. For example, let's say a court card shows up in the "foundation of a relationship" position. This card represents the quality that the relationship has, versus a particular person in the relationship.

So, when a court card appears, ask your inner guidance:

- Is this a person in the questioner's life?
- Is this an aspect of the questioner?
- Does this card embody some quality that will help the questioner?
- Is this a quality of some energies around the questioner?

As we dive into the court cards, it's useful to think of them as families. While a bit more simplistic than real-life families, we will see the general characteristics of the suit and how they relate to each of the family roles.

[12]

The Swords Family

The members of the Swords family are the intellectuals, thinkers, and communicators. From an astrological perspective, they represent the air signs—Gemini, Libra, and Aquarius—and those air sign qualities. They are fast, quick-thinking, witty, alert, and tend to be somewhat emotionally detached and more analytical in their approach to life. They are curious and great at coming up with fresh new ideas. Generally decisive and diplomatic, they may have an ease in social situations or, equally, can remain up in their heads.

Your Adventure with the Page of Swords

Page of Swords

The Page of Swords shows a young man with a sword raised. He's stepping forward but looking back over his shoulder. There are large fluffy clouds in the sky behind him, as well as a flock of birds. The winds whip his ponytail back and the trees in the distance are being blown about. Beneath his feet, the undulating ground looks almost like a striped scarf blowing in the breeze.

The Page of Swords embodies the freshness of youth *and* air; the beautiful quality that a windy spring day has when it kicks up all the dust and sweeps it out. Even though he is alert and ready for any attack, he is holding his sword a bit awkwardly. He doesn't have the mastery of his tools yet. This Page can have a somewhat impulsive and reckless nature—a bold "let me jump in and I'll figure it out as I go along" improvisational quality, and he will land on his feet more often than not. If he falls, he's resilient and will pick himself back up quickly. Even though he is bold, that "stepping forward but looking back" gesture means that once he jumps in, he may second-guess himself simply due to lack of experience.

The Page of Swords is not afraid of new or untested methods. He's willing to try something out to see if it works and will likely be an innovator and an early adopter of the newest technology. As a page, he is the ultimate communicator and loves word play and witty verbal humor. He will communicate at his best using technologies such as texting and messaging, and stand out with his thought-provoking, subversively humorous posts on social media. He doesn't mind stirring things up and debating others, like the wind whipping those trees and his hair around, but he always does so with intelligence and wit.

The Keys to the Treasure Chest—
Key Symbols of the Page of Swords

Clouds—dreamy, willing to venture into the unknown

Flock of birds—free, connected to other free spirits

Ground beneath his feet—not particularly concerned with stability

Rolling hills—challenges are easily conquered

Stepping forward but looking back—early adopter, questions actions after the fact

Sword raised—lack of experience, using new technology

Trees—resiliency, adaptability

Wind—impulsive, adaptable, communicator

Young man—eagerness, innocence

The Wizard's Words of Wisdom—
What the Page of Swords Signifies in a Reading

Being a spontaneous go-getter

Being an early adopter of technology

Communicating fresh ideas

Enthusiastic and original thinking

Possessing an eagerness and quick wit

Behind the Mysterious Door—Journal Question
to Explore the Page of Swords More Deeply

What preconceived notions am I ready to release?

Magic Words—Affirmation for the Page of Swords

"I approach life with freshness and enthusiasm."

Your Adventure with the Knight of Swords

Knight of Swords

A young man in a full suit of armor charges into battle on a white horse. The red feathers at the top of his helmet fly back in the wind as his horse jumps over a small hill at a full gallop. Over his armor, the Knight wears a surcoat decorated with a bird pattern and his horse's reins and trappings are decorated with birds and butterflies. In the background, a strong wind blows the trees and scatters the clouds into jagged patches, while a small flock of birds wheels overhead.

The Knight of Swords is charging into the battle at full speed. It's clear from his expression that he has every intention of taking out the enemy in battle no matter what the cost. While all knights have an element of courage, this Knight is the true warrior. But make no mistake, warriors are not fearless. Being fearless means not being in touch with the reality that there are risks. Being fearless is insanity. Instead, a warrior is *courageous*. Courage means that you have been trained and you let your preparation carry you through scary situations. Think of firefighters, for example. They go through the training and preparation so that when they are confronted with a burning building, they can push through their natural hesitation and drop into action. In other words, they "feel the fear and do it anyway."

If the circumstances seem daunting, but what you want is "over there," the way to get to your good stuff is by pushing through that fear and relying on your preparation, which is your armor. It doesn't have to be about combat or life or death situations. Maybe you want to ask that cute coworker out on a date, or maybe you want to apply to the college of your dreams, or perhaps it's giving stand-up comedy a go. We want what's on the other side (the lover, the education, the applause) but the way to get there feels really, really scary. If the Knight of Swords shows up in your reading, he's telling you to take out your sword, spur your horse on, stop dreaming, and go for it.

This Knight is also the "knight in shining armor" that we all want in our lives. While sometimes this card shows up as someone who is coming to the rescue to defend us, it can also mean that we need to advocate for ourselves, to stand up and speak out about what we know is right. This Knight reminds us that the time to speak our truth is now.

The Keys to the Treasure Chest— Key Symbols of the Knight of Swords

Armor—battle-ready, protection, preparation

Bare right hand—audacity, baring it all

Birds in sky—charging forward without knowing all the details

Burgundy cape—practical, mundane experience means preparation

Jagged clouds—confusion being blown away, clarity

Knight—courage, daring, risk-taking

Open helmet—alert, aware, brave

Red feathers—reaching up to connect to divine energy, conscious enlightenment

Red glove on left hand—keeping one hand on physical experience

Small hill—obstacles are minimal and easily overcome

Surcoat with bird pattern—freedom, "flightiness," speed, agility

Trappings with birds and butterflies—swiftness, control, evolution, transformation

White horse—being the chosen one for the task, having special skills

Wind—adaptability, force, using thought and logic

The Wizard's Words of Wisdom—
What the Knight of Swords Signifies in a Reading

A knight in shining armor

Feeling the fear and doing it anyway

Fortitude in the face of daunting circumstances

Impulsive action

Others defending you or advocating for yourself

Behind the Mysterious Door—Journal Questions
to Explore the Knight of Swords More Deeply

What do I fear? What action can I take to push through
this fear?

Magic Words—Affirmation for the Knight of Swords

"I am a courageous, peaceful warrior."

Your Adventure with the Queen of Swords

Queen of Swords

A queen sits on a throne holding an upright sword in her right hand. On her left hand, she wears a bracelet of prayer beads. She reaches out in a welcoming gesture, but her expression is stern. She wears a cloak with a cloud pattern on it and a yellow crown of butterflies. Her throne is decorated with a winged cherub's head, butterflies, and waxing and waning crescent moons.

One of the things that sums up this card better than anything else is the Queen's relationship to the clouds in the background. This is a woman whose head is definitely *not* in the clouds. In fact, the clouds may be all around her, including on her cape, but her head, her sword, and her upraised hand emerge from the clouds into the clear blue sky. She is a just, fair, decisive, and clearheaded woman.

That sword pointing straight up is reminiscent of the Ace of Swords and its pure intention of clarity. She is gazing with confidence and directness. While she may be holding the sword of strength and justice in her right hand, the hand of logic and authority, she is also extending the intuitive and receiving left hand in compassion and mercy. She is a seeker of absolute truth. The single bird above her represents her ability to see the facts from a higher viewpoint and look for the one single truth.

Swords are also about defining clear boundaries, and when this card shows up in a reading, it can indicate the need for drawing those logical and clearly spelled out boundaries within ourselves or with others. The cherub is a head with no body, and the Queen of Swords is definitely at home up in her head.

Because the court cards in the Swords family are about clarity and communication and Queens are leaders, we often see this card showing up when writing is highlighted, whether it's writing in a journal to gain insight and wisdom or writing that magnum opus novel you've always wanted to create. Like the angel, moons, and butterflies on her stone throne, she is able to take the mystical, dreamy, and spiritual, and translate them for others to understand.

The Keys to the Treasure Chest—
Key Symbols of the Queen of Swords

Bird—freedom, autonomy, one truth

Bracelet of prayer beads—compassion, mercy, caring

Butterflies—evolution, transformation

Cherub's head—angelic blessings, working in divine realms

Cloud cloak—comfortable defining hazy areas, gives clarity to mystery

Clouds—head out of the clouds, logical clarity, objectivity

Crescent moons—working in the world of mystery, expansion, and release

Gray gown—unafraid of dealing with "gray areas"

Queen—compassionate judgment, writer, clear communicator

Red veil and shoes—feet on the ground, thoughts on practical matters

Stern expression—confidence, poise, self-assuredness, being direct

Stream—movement, change, life

Throne—empowered decider, recognized authority

Trees—growth, reaching for the sky

Upright sword—decisiveness, judgment, defined boundaries, communication

Welcoming gesture—connecting to others, sharing

Yellow butterfly crown—divine connection, metamorphosis

The Wizard's Words of Wisdom—
What the Queen of Swords Signifies in a Reading

A fair and even-handed authority figure

A truth-seeker

Drawing clear boundaries

Impartial judgment

Written communication

Behind the Mysterious Door—Journal Question
to Explore the Queen of Swords More Deeply

How can I draw clear boundaries in this situation?

Magic Words—Affirmation for the Queen of Swords

"I have clarity and see the truth."

Your Adventure with the King of Swords

King of Swords

A king holding a sword sits face forward on a high-backed throne decorated with butterflies, crescent moons, and a beautiful fairy. In his right hand, he holds an upright sword, while his left hand rests on his lap. He wears a golden crown decorated with butterfly wings and a winged cherub.

The King of Swords is the leader who uses his analytical powers to come up with solutions. The King looks directly at us, his sword tilted slightly to the right, showing that he leans toward solutions that require action and follow-through, not just cool observation and playing with ideas. The ring on the middle finger of his left hand is symbolic. The middle finger in palmistry is the Saturn finger and represents control, authority, and discernment—a ring on this finger highlights these characteristics.

Although he holds a sword in his hand, his blue gown indicates that his mission is tranquility and peace. His red hood represents that his primary mental concern is issues on the earthly plane rather than spiritual matters. The crown on his head establishes his divinely ordained authority, while the butterflies on his crown and throne indicate a calling to transform humanity. The fairy looking over his left shoulder indicates that while he may use logic to resolve issues, he has the support of the supernatural world.

Like the Queen, his head is above the clouds, and with the two birds to his left, he can take the analysis from his higher viewpoint and communicate it to others in ways they can understand. Those birds also indicate that he may be able to see things from more than one angle and reconcile differing viewpoints. The King of Swords is a person of ideas, and while not always the one to take action himself, he can be an inspiration to others and influence them to take action on his ideas.

The Keys to the Treasure Chest—
Key Symbols of the King of Swords

> Butterflies—transformation, evolution
>
> Cherub—spiritual guidance
>
> Clouds—head above the clouds, clarity
>
> Crescent moons—ability to translate the unknowable
>
> Crown—divine authority, connection to Spirit
>
> Fairy—supernatural support
>
> King—authority, intellect, reason
>
> Pale blue gown—tranquility, peace
>
> Red cowl—mind on matters in the physical experience
>
> Red sleeves and shoe—grounded in earthly issues, authority over the mundane
>
> Ring on middle finger—control, discernment
>
> Sword—ideas leading to action
>
> Tall trees—reaching higher
>
> Throne—high ethics, standards
>
> Two birds—translation, reconciling multiple realities

The Wizard's Words of Wisdom—
What the King of Swords Signifies in a Reading

> A solutions-oriented problem solver
>
> A transforming visionary
>
> A translator of high spiritual ideals
>
> Critical discernment
>
> Reconciling two differing points of view

Behind the Mysterious Door—Journal Questions to Explore the King of Swords More Deeply

What two viewpoints do I hold simultaneously? How can I reconcile them?

Magic Words—Affirmation for the King of Swords

"I solve problems with ease."

[13]

The Wands Family

The members of the Wands family are the ones who take action, create, and live life with intensity and passion. In the astrological realm, they represent the fire signs—Aries, Leo, and Sagittarius—and those fire sign qualities. The members of this family are go-getters who live large. They have big hearts and a fearless thirst for adventure. Enthusiasm and a zest for life are the hallmark of Wands people. With all their energy, they are generally proactive but can get themselves in a pickle at times if they act without a clear plan in mind. They're not so much talkers or dreamers, but rather spirited doers, and generally attract others with their warmth and generosity.

Your Adventure with the Page of Wands

Page of Wands

The redheaded Page of Wands stands in the deserts of Egypt in front of the Pyramids of Giza. He holds a staff in his hand and gazes at it in wonder. He wears a yellow tunic covered in a stylized salamander pattern, tan boots with flame-shaped fringe, and a little short-brimmed hat with a small red feather.

The Page of Wands is the enthusiastic beginner. He is just at the start of his journey and is fascinated with the brand-new wand he has been given. What he lacks in experience on the job, he makes up for in enthusiasm and interest. This young messenger is willing to explore exotic territory, not only for the wisdom gained, but also for the thrill of the adventure. The small red feather in his cap indicates that the passionate fire burning within him is a small but growing flame reaching up to connect with Spirit. The salamander pattern on his tunic is the elemental animal of fire. Although we know now that salamanders are amphibians, when salamanders crept out of rotting logs thrown on the fire, ancient people believed that they were born of fire and able to withstand heat and flame. This animal with the spirit of fire can withstand the heat of intense passion.

The Page of Wands represents new, passionate undertakings, particularly those with a physically active or creatively dynamic energy to them. This Page will jump in with enthusiasm, especially if it is into something that has never been experienced before. There is a youthful aspect to the Page of Wands that can show up as bubbly exuberance. He can also show up in our lives as the enthusiastic cheerleader or supportive sidekick, like the Robin to our Batman.

The Keys to the Treasure Chest—
Key Symbols of the Page of Wands

Desert—fiery heat, exotic locales

Orange leggings—the ability to push through blocks, will and energy

Page—enthusiastic messages, beginner

Pyramids of Giza—adventure, spiritual mystery

Salamander—the strength to withstand the heat of competition

Small red feather—small but growing flame of spiritual connection

Staff—passion, eagerness

Tan boots and cape—connection to material creation

Yellow tunic—success orientation

The Wizard's Words of Wisdom—
What the Page of Wands Signifies in a Reading

A dynamic creator

A passionate doer

A supportive sidekick

Enthusiastic exploration

Spirited curiosity

Behind the Mysterious Door—Journal Question
to Explore the Page of Wands More Deeply

What new things do I want to explore?

Magic Words—Affirmation for the Page of Wands

"I am passionate about new adventures."

Your Adventure with the Knight of Wands

Knight of Wands

The Knight of Wands sits on a russet horse rearing up on its hind legs. He wears a full suit of armor, covered with a yellow tunic printed with salamanders. His horse's trappings are green with small yellow leaves printed on them. The hem of the Knight's tunic, the red feather on his helmet, and the red cape on his back resemble flames. Both of his hands are gloved—his right holds a short staff while the left holds the reins. He is also in the Egyptian desert with the three Pyramids of Giza in the background.

The Knight of Wands represents sexy charisma and wild wanderlust. The energy of this Knight is of the charismatic explorer and the sexual adventurer. His feisty horse is rearing up as though mounting a mare, the wand in his hand has a definite phallic quality, and his clothes make him look like he's on fire! This Knight is irresistible to others and uses his charisma not only to attract lovers, but also to convince others to join his causes or accompany him on his adventures.

His adventurousness extends beyond the bedroom though—and would hardly be limited to the bedroom anyway! The exotic locale indicates this Knight is a nomadic wanderer, never staying in one place for any length of time. The new sprouting leaves on his horse's trappings indicate that he is a seeker who longs for novel experiences, either trying out different careers, traveling the world, or going from one creative or active endeavor to another.

Like the Page of Wands, the Knight of Wands thrives in the world of physical or creative exploration, but he tends to bring more energy that is connected to others. Networking is his specialty, both personally and professionally.

The Keys to the Treasure Chest—
Key Symbols of the Knight of Wands

Armor—protection, safety, preparation

Desert—uncultivated and unexplored land, willingness to explore unknown territory

Gloves—travel, defense

Green trappings with leaves—new life, animation

Horse—sexuality, vigor

Knight—courage, connecting to others, adventurousness

Pyramids of Giza—unusual connection to divine energy, exotic experiences

Red feather and cape—fire, sexual heat

Salamander print—adaptability, resilience

Staff—sexual attraction, fiery passion, will

Yellow tunic—success orientation, victory

The Wizard's Words of Wisdom—
What the Knight of Wands Signifies in a Reading

A charismatic networker

A creative connector

Nomadic wandering

Novel experiences

Sexual adventure

Behind the Mysterious Door—
Journal Question to Explore the Knight of Wands More Deeply

What could networking with others offer me?

Magic Words—Affirmation for the Knight of Wands

"I am open to connections with new people."

Your Adventure with the Queen of Wands

Queen of Wands

The Queen of Wands holds a staff in one hand and a sunflower in the other. She sits with her legs apart on a throne with lion-shaped armrests and an orange tapestry embroidered with sunflowers and lions decorating the back. Her crown is gold with emerald leaves sprouting from the top. A black cat sits at her feet. In the distance we see a desert and the three Pyramids of Giza.

The Queen of Wands has the strength and pride of a lion and the gregarious extroversion of the sunflower. Like the sunflower, she follows the light—she is someone who reflects positivity and warmth. She is upfront with her emotions—both the positive ones and the more volatile ones. It's all out there in the open. She represents passion and the position of her legs, while not as forceful as the Knight of Wands, represents an openness about sexuality. She is the kind of person who is secure in her success and translates that into support for others. The black cat in front of her represents the fact that the Queen is protected from spiritual harm. It also represents her ability to get whatever she is aiming for, just as a cat goes out and catches mice. The pyramids in the distance are less prominent, almost an afterthought. She is a worldly woman who has experience with many cultures and so flows comfortably and easily in groups outside of her own culture. She is seated on a platform, showing that she is a bit removed from the harshness of life.

The Keys to the Treasure Chest—
Key Symbols of the Queen of Wands

Black cat—protection, ability

Crown—divine connection, authority is divinely ordained

Desert—easily adapts to unusual places

Leaves—growth orientation, freshness

Legs apart—comfortable with her sexuality

Lions—courage, ferocity

Orange tapestry—pushing through blocks

Platform—distanced from harsh environments

Pyramids of Giza—experienced with multiple cultures, culturally well versed

Queen—facilitator, connected to others, community-oriented

Staff—passionate emotions, sexually aware

Sunflowers—openness with emotions, positivity

White cloak—high spiritual motivation

Yellow gown—success, fame

The Wizard's Words of Wisdom—
What the Queen of Wands Signifies in a Reading

A charismatic extrovert

An assertive self-starter

Being sexually comfortable

Freely showing all emotions

Reflecting growth and positivity

Behind the Mysterious Door—Journal Question
to Explore the Queen of Wands More Deeply

How can I bring more of my emotions out into the open?

Magic Words—Affirmation for the Queen of Wands

"I get whatever I aim for."

Your Adventure with the King of Wands

King of Wands

The King of Wands sits on a throne looking to the left with a large wooden staff loosely held in his right hand. He wears a red robe, a yellow cape decorated with a salamander pattern, a golden lion pendant, and a golden crown decorated with flame shapes. His throne is covered with a lion and salamander design. On the platform next to him, his salamander companion rests at his side.

His throne rests on a platform that lifts him up above the desert floor and carries him above the mundane concerns of life. He doesn't allow his passion to control him, he controls his passions—both sexual and in temperament. The salamander companion at his side watches to the west too. While neither seem alarmed, they are alert and prepared. The salamander image on his throne is biting its own tail and forms a complete circle. This circle is a symbol of infinity and also of maturity—of "coming full circle." Compare these to the salamanders on the Knight's and Page's clothing that are curled but do not form a complete circle.

The King's crown rests over his soft helmet and its points are shaped like tongues of flame, indicating that his thoughts are focused on creativity and action.

The lions on his necklace and the tapestry behind him represent strength, courage, and authority. His staff is being held loosely, indicating that he isn't being too precious about his talent. He is confident and not fearful of losing control.

The Keys to the Treasure Chest—
Key Symbols of the King of Wands

Crown with flame shapes—inspired, creative thoughts, active thinker

Green cape with yellow robe—connection with life and growth, success

Helmet—protection from burning temptation

King—authority, top-down leadership

Lions—strength, nobility

Red robe—dominion over sensuality and earthly pleasures

Salamanders—true faith, the ability to withstand passionate temptation

Staff held loosely—confidence in his talent and abilities

Throne on platform—removed from the mundane

The Wizard's Words of Wisdom—
What the King of Wands Signifies in a Reading

A prepared and alert leader

Channeling passion into action

Coming full circle

Confident and controlled emotions

Someone who has mastered his sexual appetites

Behind the Mysterious Door—Journal Question
to Explore the King of Wands More Deeply

How can I channel passion into action?

Magic Words—Affirmation for the King of Wands

"I guide myself to my most productive emotions."

[14]

The Cups Family

The members of the Cups family are the dreamers, the psychics, the creators of imaginative and introspective art, and the spiritually connected, metaphysical ones. They are the souls who can easily navigate the world of emotions and dive in deeply. In the astrological realm, they represent the water signs—Cancer, Scorpio, and Pisces—and those water sign qualities. The members of this family are feelers, intuitives, and dreamers. They are the empaths who can pick up the emotions and energies around them. They also tend to have a rich inner life that they protect jealously. This may show up as having a hidden side, being secretive, or simply being more introverted than most. If they are able to find an outlet, they can feel safe revealing this hidden self through art that allows them to express what I call the "poetic" emotions, as opposed to the fiery emotions of the wands. They are also deeply attuned to the mystical world. They are spiritually oriented and naturally gravitate to and understand the sacred mysteries. They tend to be rather adaptable and fluid. Changeability is both their strength and their weakness. Their connection to the dream world can make them exceptionally romantic in relationships, ascribing all kinds of mystical significance to love.

Your Adventure with the Page of Cups

Page of Cups

A young man stands in front of an ocean with rolling waves holding a golden goblet with a fish coming out of it. He is wearing a light blue turban that resembles flowing water, a pink puffy sleeved shirt, and a light blue tunic with lotuses on it.

Have you ever heard the fairytale of "The Fisherman and His Wife?" In it, a fisherman catches and then releases a talking fish who grants him wishes. I always think of this story when the Page of Cups makes an appearance. Here he is, standing in front of the rolling waves of the sea, seemingly having a conversation with his pet fish, who he's holding up in a cup. I love the magic of fairytales where animals, immortals, and even trees and rocks talk, so of course, I adore this card. It seems natural that a member of the Cups family with all its connection to the magic of the spirit world would have a friendship with an animal from the spiritual depths of the sea.

The Cups' element of water is about the quieter, more internal emotions and the Page represents the communication of those emotions. It's as if the Page and the fish, looking into each other's eyes, could communicate telepathically. The Page of Cups represents someone who is skilled at this kind of non-verbal communication. That fish also indicates that, with the subject at hand, working psychically may be the most effective mode. The Page also has a childlike intuition, open and uninhibited. You may find that if you are dealing with a Page of Cups person, they'll blurt out exactly what *you're* thinking, whether it's appropriate or not.

His watery hat resembles an overflowing bowl with water splashing out and symbolizes the profuse emotion that is consuming his thoughts. As an immature person who lacks emotional experience, he lets his feelings override his good judgment using his heart over his head. He may not yet understand that the ups and downs of the water behind him are the feelings that come and go, get stronger at times, and other times fade away. He believes whatever emotion he's feeling in the moment is forever.

But this Page isn't just all about emotion, the spiritual aspect of the Cups is also expressed here. The lotuses on his tunic are a reminder that spiritual enlightenment emerges from earthy experiences. Reaching for enlightenment is also an important aspect of this card, but as the Page is a student and beginner, he may just be awakening to that awareness.

The Keys to the Treasure Chest— Key Symbols of the Page of Cups

Cup—internalized emotions, spirituality, intuition

Fish—psychic communication, body language

Ocean waves—emotions going up and down

Page—youthfulness, beginner, spiritual student

Pink shirt and leggings—sweet and naive romance

Tunic with lotuses—reaching for enlightenment

Watery turban—emotions controlling thoughts, love on one's mind, heart over head

The Wizard's Words of Wisdom— What the Page of Cups Signifies in a Reading

A person who wears their heart on their sleeve

Emotional ups and downs

Innocent intuition

Psychic connection

Someone who is just awakening to spiritual enlightenment

Behind the Mysterious Door—Journal Question to Explore the Page of Cups More Deeply

What new spiritual idea am I just discovering?

Magic Words—Affirmation for the Page of Cups

"I am intuitive and psychically aware."

Your Adventure with the Knight of Cups

Knight of Cups

A young man dressed in armor on a gray horse is about to cross a stream. He carries a golden chalice in front of him. His helmet and boots are decorated with silver wings and he wears a surcoat embroidered with red fish and wavy water patterns.

I always see the Knight of Cups as a knight in search of the Holy Grail. The Arthurian knights were often sent on quests with important missions to fulfill and in many versions of these stories, they were sent to find the cup that Jesus used at the Last Supper. Scholars trace these Grail stories back to even older Celtic myths of magic vessels that, once used, would satisfy all thirst and hunger. Whether you ascribe the Grail to Christian or Celtic lore, it's most definitely a magic cup that brings miracles. So, while the Page of Cups is just beginning to get the concept of enlightenment, the Knight is on a mission and actively searching for it. If every knight in the tarot is concerned with attaining goals, then the goal of the Knight of Cups is spiritual awakening.

His winged hat and boots are reminiscent of the Greek god Hermes, the messenger of Mount Olympus and the guide for dead souls traveling to the underworld. Even the stream the Knight crosses is reminiscent of the River Styx, the river that all souls must cross in the afterlife. This Knight shares those qualities with Hermes, bringing divine messages and assistance to those in need. The Knight of Cups is an open-hearted spiritual helper, someone who can channel messages from spirit guides or easily venture into the spirit realm.

His armor indicates that he is a spiritual/emotional adventurer who is willing to enter into risky situations, while his fishy surcoat and the watery trappings on his horse show that he has the ability to dive deeply into the world of the heart and emotions. The Knight of Cups is someone who is ready to go on the adventure of love, romantic or otherwise. That means experiencing deeper feelings than he has ever experienced before. He not only wants to experience these feelings himself, but also wants to lead others to those deeper feelings, too.

The Keys to the Treasure Chest—
Key Symbols of the Knight of Cups

Armor—protection, preparation

Cup—heart, deep emotions, spirituality

Gray horse—slow, steady movement, gray areas, undefined energy

Helmet and boots with wings—bringing divine messages

Knight—daring, spiritual adventurer

Mountains—reaching higher peaks of enlightenment

Red fish and water pattern—sensuality is entwined with deep emotion

Stream—crossing over to the other side, traveling easily between the worlds

Trees—growth before attainment

The Wizard's Words of Wisdom—
What the Knight of Cups Signifies in a Reading

A heart-connected helper

A person who has the highest spiritual intentions

Being on a sacred quest

Going on the adventure of love

Someone who delivers divine messages from the realm of Spirit

Behind the Mysterious Door—Journal Question
to Explore the Knight of Cups More Deeply

What is my highest spiritual intention?

Magic Words—Affirmation for the Knight of Cups

"I bravely open my heart to love."

Your Adventure with the Queen of Cups

Queen of Cups

A queen sits on a heavy stone throne at the edge of a pebble-covered beach. The calmly swirling waters seem to be rising and surrounding her, even touching the bottom of her white gown. She wears a cape with a watery design that is held together with a shell-shaped clasp. Her throne is decorated with baby mermaids holding a fish and a large scallop shell. She herself holds a large ornate chalice with a lid in both hands. A little fish sits on the beach beside her.

The Queen of Cups is the ultimate caretaker. She is someone so deeply empathetic that she can identify what someone else needs even before they do. If you grew up with a parent who was lavish in their loving affection, you also get an idea of this Queen's energy. She's the ultimate mom, and one who can read your mind at that!

The chalice that she holds is unique. It is the only one in the deck with a cover on it and instead of being round, it's hexagonal. If the chalice represents spiritual wisdom, then this cover symbolizes that this Queen is the keeper of very deep, mysterious esoteric knowledge. Like a psychic mystic, she is gazing at the chalice as if she has X-ray vision and can see what's inside, even if we can't. There is a cross at the top of the lid, angels inscribed on the panels of the cup, and two kneeling angel figures on the arms on either side. These angels are very similar to the description of the Ark of the Covenant in the Bible, which was the chest that held the tablets of the Ten Commandments. Whatever secret is held inside this cup, it is clearly one worthy of angelic protection. When I first discovered the tarot as a child, I had a tiny deck with poor reproductions of the images. When I looked at the Queen of Cups' chalice, I used to see two mechanical crab claws, rather than two angels. My childlike intuition made a strange association and why I thought two robotic crab claws would be attached to a chalice, I'll never know. Nevertheless, that misinterpretation is an interesting one. The angels are there as protection and crabs use their claws to defend themselves. The Queen of Cups corresponds to the sun sign Cancer the crab and since I am a Cancer myself, perhaps I was able to use that dreamy, watery instinct to tune into this energy. While the angels protect the cup, the water babies hold a protective scallop shell at the top of the throne, guarding the Queen herself. All these signs of protection are a reminder that empaths—people who can easily connect to the emotions of others—have to be careful to also safeguard themselves. The cliffs behind her also represent a natural barrier, but in this case it means knowing that the universe shelters her and she has nothing to fear.

There are beautifully colored pebbles and gemstones at the Queen's feet. Those polished stones represent the patience and power of water. By tumbling them gently over thousands of years, they become beautiful talismans of nature. The Queen of Cups is also someone who has the patience to see results come over time.

The water babies on her throne represent her fertility, her ability to give birth to and nurture projects (or actual babies) that connect her to deeper spiritual wisdom.

Her little fish companion is her spirit animal. It represents her adaptability and her vulnerability.

The Keys to the Treasure Chest— Key Symbols of the Queen of Cups

Angels—angelic protection, connection to the spirit world

Baby mermaids—children, caring for others

Beach—easily moving between the material and spiritual worlds

Chalice with lid—hidden secrets of the heart, sacred mysteries

Cliff—naturally protected from the world

Crown—divinely ordained authority, crown chakra connection

Fish—adaptable, vulnerable

Queen—nurturer, emotional caretaker

Rising waters—emotions and spirituality taking over your consciousness

Shells—safety for empaths

Stones—gemstone work, patience

Throne—knowing your own worth, poise

Watery cape—connected to the realm of dreams and psyche

White gown—spiritual concerns

The Wizard's Words of Wisdom— What the Queen of Cups Signifies in a Reading

A nurturing caretaker

A self-protective empath

Guardian of sacred mysteries

Psychic mastery

Secrets of the heart

Behind the Mysterious Door—Journal Question to Explore the Queen of Cups More Deeply

What mysteries do I hold inside that I show no one except myself?

Magic Words—Affirmation for the Queen of Cups

"I have the patience to polish the gemstones I hold inside me."

Your Adventure with the King of Cups

KING of CUPS.

King of Cups

The King of Cups sits on a throne on a platform in the middle of the ocean. He sits calmly even though he is surrounded by waves on all sides. He holds a chalice in his right hand and a lotus-shaped scepter in his left, which echoes the lotus decoration on his throne and crown. He wears fish scale boots and around his neck he wears a golden fish medallion. In the background, a fish jumps out of the water and in the distance a ship with red sails navigates the waves.

With his throne on a stone slab, the King of Cups is the most structured of the Cups family. He sits calmly in the middle of the ocean even with the restless waves around him. This is someone who understands his feelings and is able to ride out the emotional ups and downs and create a sense of stability. Unlike the fickle Page, the King is adaptable but knows that feelings ebb and flow and doesn't act on those moment-to-moment emotions.

The lotus scepter, throne, and crown establish him as someone who has attained spiritual enlightenment. Unlike the Page who was just getting the first inklings of this connection to divine wisdom, the King has found the doorway and has entered into the deepest realms of ancient spiritual knowledge. His worldly authority comes from his sacred enlightenment.

The fish medallion and fish scale boots indicate that he is someone who is comfortable with the vulnerability of emotion, while the fish jumping out of the water shows that opening his heart brings him happiness. Our little fish has moved from being in the Page's cup, to an emblem for the Knight, to the shore next to the Queen, and, finally, to joy and freedom in the ocean beside the King. This is a subtle message that the more we connect to the divine, the happier and freer we will be.

The red in his cloak and crown demonstrate that while he may be spiritually connected, he still enjoys the sensual aspects of the world and the helmet reflects his ability to protect himself without being overly guarded. The red-sailed ship navigating the waves is a symbol of his ability to use his kind-hearted compassion to his advantage, creating effective change for himself or others.

The Keys to the Treasure Chest— Key Symbols of the King of Cups

Cup—emotionally aware, comfortable with emotion

Fish—comfort with vulnerability, joy, freedom

King —material world authority, calm and established

Light blue gown—calm, tranquility, composure

Light blue helmet—feeling safe

Lotus—total enlightenment, complete spiritual connection

Ocean waves—Serene amongst the deepest emotions and spiritual experiences

Platform—rooted in tradition

Red and green cloak—linking to the material world

Sailing ship with red sails—creating large-scale change

The Wizard's Words of Wisdom— What the King of Cups Signifies in a Reading

A leader with emotional depth

A spiritual traditionalist

Connecting the sensual and spiritual

Enlightenment leading to joy

Serenity in vulnerability

Behind the Mysterious Door—Journal Question to Explore the King of Cups More Deeply

What spiritual work can I do to bring in more joy?

Magic Words—Affirmation for the King of Cups

"I dive deeply into my emotions to bring up the very best feelings."

[15]

The Pentacles Family

The members of the Pentacles family are the pragmatic realists, the steady builders, the real-world producers, the abundant earners, and the practical visionaries. They are the ones who know how the material world works and can solve problems and see long-term projects through to completion. In the astrological realm, the Pentacles family represents the earth signs—Taurus, Virgo, and Capricorn—and those earth sign qualities.

The members of this family are traditional, responsible, and love routine and stability. They are the achievers who, once they find a worthy project, will make a plan and then follow each step till it is complete—or if it's something that is ongoing, continue on with it forever. Like the Wands family, they are doers, but whereas the Wands folks will happily drop something if they find a new project that they like better, the Pentacles have a hard time shifting gears once they get started and definitely don't feel comfortable "winging it." With all those prominent gold discs, the Pentacles family is concerned with money and possessions—not only for being luxuriously wealthy, but also because stability and having a safety net is so important to them. The Pentacles family members tend to "save for a rainy day" in all areas, not just money. They work toward efficiency in how they spend their time and energy. They are connected to the body, health, and physicality—especially when it comes to pleasures. More than any other suit, they know how to enjoy all the earthly delights.

Your Adventure with the Page of Pentacles

Page of Pentacles

The Page of Pentacles stands in a green, grassy meadow above a small plowed field admiring a golden pentacle that he holds up with both hands. He is dressed in brown and green but wears an elaborate red turban atop his head.

The Page of Pentacles is the most practical of all the Pages. He may be just starting his journey to finding purpose in life, but he has a plan on how to get there. I think of this Page as being like that kid in high school who knew what she was going to do for her career, had her first choice college picked out, and was already thinking about where she was going to work when she was finished.

With his big gold coin, the Page of Pentacles is going to buy that small plot of land and plow and plant the seeds of his project. He is making his first investment. When the Page of Pentacles shows up in a reading, it indicates that someone is at the start of a long-term project. He may be a student or a true beginner at something, but he has prepared for this moment and takes it seriously. The Page is wearing a red turban to indicate his love of sensual indulgences. He is already planning on how he's going to enjoy the profits he makes from his investment, but the brown and green of his outfit symbolize his grounded practical nature and his ability to make his investment grow.

His gesture supports this. He is holding the golden disc with reverence. He appreciates the opportunity that he has been given and he's not going to waste it. As young as he is, he knows the value of what he is receiving.

The small flowers at his feet reflect the help that nature will provide in the process. The small grove of trees indicates that there are still untapped areas of possibility for the future. The mountain indicates that there may be bigger opportunities ahead, but they are distant. Because the Pages all indicate communication, this card in a reading can indicate getting some good news about your finances or your health.

The Keys to the Treasure Chest—
Key Symbols of the Page of Pentacles

Brown shirt, leggings, and boots—grounded in reality

Distant mountain—climbing the heights in the future

Grassy meadow and flowers—prosperity is just sprouting

Green tunic—growth oriented

Page—apprenticeship, a beginner with a plan

Pentacle—material wealth, health

Red turban—mind is on material gain

Small grove of trees—finding your way through confusion

Small plowed field—beginning his investment in the future

The Wizard's Words of Wisdom—
What the Page of Pentacles Signifies in a Reading

A beginner with foresight

Attending to foundational practical matters

Being given a leg up

Taking advantage of new opportunities

Taking the first steps in your plan

Behind the Mysterious Door—Journal Questions
to Explore the Page of Pentacles More Deeply

What is my long-term goal? What first step do I need to take to get there?

Magic Words—Affirmation for the Page of Pentacles

"Taking my first steps will lead me to my goal."

Your Adventure with the Knight of Pentacles

KNIGHT of PENTACLES.

Knight of Pentacles

A knight sits on his black horse at a standstill atop a grassy hill. He holds his golden disc in a gloved hand but looks past it toward the large plowed field beyond. He wears a suit of armor with a red-and-black striped surcoat. He and his horse both wear oak leaves instead of a plume and his horse's trappings have a stylized oak leaf pattern.

The Knight of Pentacles is the diligent workhorse. Someone who knows the value of sticking with one thing and seeing it through to the end. When he shows up in a reading, he's a reminder that if you stick to the plan, you'll see the end result and the rewards will be even better than you're expecting. He's the tortoise in the fable "The Tortoise and the Hare." He knows that steady, small actions done over time will produce results. His black horse is at a complete standstill. It's interesting to note the relationships between the riders and the horses in the images of the four Knights. The Knight of Swords has a horse that's galloping as fast as he can. The Knight of Wands has a horse that's rearing up—active but not quite as forceful as the Knight of Swords' horse. The Knight of Cups' horse is walking slowly, and here we have the Knight of Pentacles standing still, almost as though he is contemplating his next move. This can, of course, indicate that there is a lack of movement, that we are stuck with all of our potential and not doing anything with it. While it may mean, "Get moving!" sometimes, it can also mean taking stock and planning before taking action. The Knight has plowed his field and now he's deciding which crops will bring him the most satisfaction and abundance.

The oak leaves on his helmet and on the horse indicate that he is building something strong and long lasting. The phrase, "Mighty oaks from little acorns grow," is a reminder that the biggest successes can start with something small. The red-and-black surcoat and trappings remind us that the twin focus of the Knight is experiencing earthly pleasure and protecting his abundance. The rough blanket under his very basic saddle shows that the Knight values practicality and frugality over flamboyance. When you're planning your next move, you may need to make small sacrifices for the greater good.

The Keys to the Treasure Chest—
Key Symbols of the Knight of Pentacles

Armor—preparation, readiness

Black horse—protection, taking stock

Distant mountain range—potential for attainment after a long journey

Glove—safety, barrier

Grass—growth, ease

Knight—guardian, champion

Oaks—long lasting, taking time, big results from small beginnings

Old brown blanket—thrift, economizing

Pentacle—practical matters, money

Plowed field—larger potential gain

Red-and-black striped surcoat—guarding material possessions

The Wizard's Words of Wisdom—
What the Knight of Pentacles Signifies in a Reading

A light at the end of the tunnel

A watchful guardian

Delaying gratification

Sticking with the plan

Taking time to build something strong

Behind the Mysterious Door—Journal Questions to Explore the Knight of Pentacles More Deeply

What is my plan? What am I doing to further this plan?

Magic Words—Affirmation for the Knight of Pentacles

"I see my project through to completion."

Your Adventure with the Queen of Pentacles

Queen of Pentacles

A queen sits on a throne in a beautiful field. In her hands she holds a golden pentacle. Around her, flowers blossom and a rose arbor in full bloom arches over her head. Her throne is decorated with images of cherubs, fruit, and a goat's head. A little rabbit runs by her feet. Her crown is decorated with a winged solar disc and a long green veil.

The Queen of Pentacles is the queen of abundance in all forms. The flowers around her, the fruit images on her throne, and the big gold coin in her hand, of course, all represent her ability to manifest the things she needs in her life with extra to spare. Where the Page and Knight were looking at abundance in the future, she is seeing abundance in the here and now. She is also the spirit of generosity. Have you ever invited friends over for dinner and had so much leftover food that you wanted them to take a plate home? That is the type of unselfish nature this Queen possesses. The fruit and flowers attest that she has more than she could ever use herself and the rabbit in the right corner represents her ability to bring in more once she gives that away. That little brown rabbit also represents her fertility. That can mean literal fertility in the form of a pregnancy or it can mean her prolific ability to create and launch projects.

This Queen doesn't give away the abundance she has created because she thinks it is worthless. Quite the opposite. She looks down at the pentacle in her hand with great contemplation. She values her gifts and sees sharing them as a way of showing her love to others.

The goat head on her throne represents the astrological sign of Capricorn, a creature that is half goat, half fish. The constellation of

Capricorn is sometimes identified with the Greek myth of Amalthea, the goat whose broken horn was transformed into the cornucopia, the horn of plenty. The cornucopia is a magical horn that endlessly produces bounty. The qualities of Capricorn also apply to the Queen of Pentacles: practical, traditional, ambitious, goal-oriented, and disciplined. When this card shows up in a reading, it is a message that these qualities will be the source of long-lasting abundance.

The Keys to the Treasure Chest— Key Symbols of the Queen of Pentacles

Cherubs—angelic protection

Crown—divine authority

Flowers—blossoming, sensual abundance

Fruit—practical abundance

Goat—cornucopia, bounty

Green veil—growth, wealth

Mountains—ability to attain higher levels of consciousness

Pentacle—knowing the value of what she shares

Queen—nurturing, financially generous

Rabbit—fertility, plenty

Red dress—connected to the senses

Rivers—flowing, thriving

Rose arbor—a gateway to understanding spirituality through the senses

White blouse—spiritually aware

Winged solar disc—divinity, goddess energy

The Wizard's Words of Wisdom—
What the Queen of Pentacles Signifies in a Reading

A generous provider

Enjoying abundance

Pleasure through the senses

Successful fertility

The ability to share with others

Behind the Mysterious Door—Journal Question
to Explore the Queen of Pentacles More Deeply

What abundance do I share with others?

Magic Words—Affirmation for the Queen of Pentacles

"Abundance comes easily to me."

Your Adventure with the King of Pentacles

King of Pentacles

On the parapet of a castle, the King of Pentacles sits on a throne carved with bull heads. His crown is covered in roses and lilies and he holds a pentacle and a scepter. He wears a red cowl and a lush robe covered in a grape pattern; leafy green plants and grapevines grow around him. His left leg and foot emerge from under his robes, clad in armor.

I remember looking at the King of Pentacles when I was first learning the tarot and thinking that he looked almost lost under that leafy, grapey gown with just his hands and face peeping out. While the Queen of Pentacles has taken her abundance and let it flow through her by sharing it with others, the King has held onto his and is in danger of drowning in it! The King of Pentacles has accumulated so much that it is bordering on excess. When this card shows up in a reading, it's a definitely a reminder to watch the balance between having enough and having too much. If you're overindulging, feeling the weight of clutter, or even hoarding, it's time to prune back and make space for the new and fresh. Donate, give away, share some of what you have gained.

The bull heads on his throne represent the astrological sign of Taurus and all of its characteristics: strength, ability to push through obstacles, dependability, and patience. The King of Pentacles didn't get this windfall overnight. He worked at it over time and as a result has created an empire that will last as long as the heavy stones of his castle.

The grapevines around him and on his gown represent abundance and enjoyment of the pleasures in life. The red cowl emphasizes the gratification he gets from his success. When we see the King of

Pentacles in a reading, the message is that you now get to enjoy the fruits of your labor.

The King has one foot emerging from his robe and it's a little peek to let us know that under that heavy robe, he is wearing a full suit of armor! He is a warrior king and has gained what he has through winning in competitive situations. He doesn't back down. He's also prepared and protected for any challenges that come his way. He's not going to give an inch. His foot is resting on a helmet. Is it *his* helmet or one that belonged to a vanquished foe? His gold crown is covered with roses and lilies, indicating that his concerns are not just in the material world. He sees the connection between material abundance and spiritual enlightenment.

The Keys to the Treasure Chest— Key Symbols of the King of Pentacles

Armor—protection, guardedness

Bull—possessive, industrious

Castle—long-lasting success

Crown—divinely conferred authority

Grapevines—plenty, affluence

Helmet—preparedness, victory

King—top-down authority, at the top of his game

Lilies—being given spiritual enlightenment

Parapet—long-lasting gains

Pentacle—material success, wealth

Plants—abundant growth

Red cowl—experiencing the world through the senses

Robes—overabundance, excess

Roses—enjoying the world through the senses

Scepter—conquering the world

The Wizard's Words of Wisdom—
What the King of Pentacles Signifies in a Reading

A competitive and victorious leader

An established traditionalist

Appreciating with the five senses

Authority in the material world

Stockpiling wealth

Behind the Mysterious Door—Journal Question
to Explore the King of Pentacles More Deeply

What successes have I achieved?

Magic Words—Affirmation for the King of Pentacles

"I am a successful and abundant leader."

[16]

Playing in the Court

While you are familiarizing yourself with the court cards, it is useful to spend some time playing with them so you can get to know them better. Separate the sixteen court cards out of the deck and try the following exercises. You can either do this with a friend or write about your choices in your tarot journal. Look over the different characters in the court cards and consciously choose the cards based on what you know about their characteristics.

1. Choose the court card that you identify with most closely.

2. Choose three cards to represent some of the different roles you take on in your life (for example: parent, employee, spouse).

3. Choose cards to represent different significant people in your life (for example: family, friends, coworkers, etc.).

4. Choose a card that embodies the qualities of something going on in your life. For example, pick a card to represent the energy of your work situation, your relationship, your health, etc.

This playtime with the court cards, just like leisure time spent with new friends, will start to open your awareness of their different personalities so you'll have a richer connection with them when they show up in a reading.

What's the Big Deal about the Major Arcana?

now we get to jump into the world of the Major Arcana. This is the big leagues, kids! The twenty-two cards that make up the Major Arcana are sometimes called trumps, which comes from the days when Tarot was a card game. In a card game, trumps are the cards that rank higher than the others. Even if you don't play cards, you might be familiar with the phrase, "that trumps everything," which is another way of saying, "that beats everything." The word "trumps" comes to us through the original name of those twenty-two cards—the "Triumphs"—and the images come to us as the allegorical archetypes meant to teach us how to navigate life in the best way possible.

The Major Arcana starts at zero and ends at twenty-one. While the Minor Arcana pips represent circumstances in our life that are more mundane, and the court cards represent people or personalities, the twenty-two Majors represent big, powerful, and even more esoteric themes. When they show up in a reading, you can expect them to have a stronger influence and impact on the situation. They may be the underlying energy that permeates the cards that surround them or offers an irresistible pull in a certain direction.

Your Adventure with The Fool

The Fool

We walk down a path and meet up with another traveler—a young man going on a journey, walking through the mountains. The sun is shining and it's a beautiful day without a cloud in the sky. He's traveling light, with a simple small pack on a stick across his shoulder and a small dog as his only companion. However, he's dressed in rich and flamboyant medieval garb, suited more for a royal rock concert than for a hike in the wilderness.

Energetically, the Fool represents young energy and enthusiasm. He also symbolizes the realization of the true limitlessness of the Universe's benevolence. The Fool is a teenager; he has just started on his journey and has his whole life ahead of him to have, do, or be whatever he can imagine. However, like many teenagers, the Fool card often gets a bad rap. Calling someone a "fool" is an insult, not a compliment. If you're a fool, you know nothing, you're an idiot. Yes, that "blank slate" quality of The Fool can be viewed as "knowing nothing," but it is much more about the limitlessness, optimism, and potential of fresh beginnings. If you really want to get down to it, the Fool actually represents the beginning *before* the beginning, the moment *before* you take your first step and begin your path. It's not an accident that this card bears the number zero. It's the tiny speck that contained the Universe right before the Big Bang—filled with the energy of amazing things yet to come.

Some tarot texts point out the fact that the Fool is gazing up at the sky while walking toward a cliff—a recipe for disaster! "If you don't pay attention to the details, you're doomed!" But the little dog beside him is the divine guidance within each of us that warns us just in the nick of time if we are headed down the wrong path. Like most teenagers, he may not think before he takes a risk but all ends well anyway. We don't see how high the cliff actually is; it could be two feet off the ground. Divine providence is always on our side and everything will work out. The Universe loves us.

The Fool is energetically the start and the end of the soul's journey through the Major Arcana. When we end one day, one activity, or even one life, there is a space between the end and the new beginning. The Fool represents this space between the finish of one and the beginning of another. This space is not about planning, preparing, or even dreaming; it's about being present in the moment and trusting that your intuition will lead you to your first step.

The Keys to the Treasure Chest— Key Symbols of The Fool

Clear sky—openness, carefree joy

Cliff—stepping into the unknown and knowing that it's going to be okay

Face up—positivity

Feather in his cap—confidence, connection to the divine, thought, "light as a feather"

Flamboyant clothing—unconcerned about judgment from others, playful, frivolous

Knapsack on a stick—traveling light, bringing along no baggage, no expectations, faith

Mountain peaks—meeting challenge head on

Sun—benevolence, divine energy, power

White dog—divine protection on your side

White rose—innocence, spirituality, blank slate quality

Young man—fresh, fun, limitless energy and enthusiasm

The Wizard's Words of Wisdom—
What The Fool Signifies in a Reading

Absolute faith and trust in the benevolence of the divine

Approaching things with a totally open mind and expecting the unexpected

Being spontaneous and following first impulses

Fearlessly following your fancy

Freedom and limitlessness

Behind the Mysterious Door—Journal Questions
to Explore The Fool More Deeply

When have you let go and trusted things to work out? What happened?

Magic Words—Affirmation for The Fool

"Life is fun."

Your Adventure with The Magician

The Magician

We meet an androgynous-looking young man standing behind a table laden with magical tools. An infinity symbol, or lemniscate, magically hovers above his head. He gestures with authority, his right hand pointing up to the sky, his left pointing down to earth. As if by magic, he makes lilies and roses grow at his feet and twine above his head.

The Magician represents uniqueness, action, focus, and creation. He is the start of all things. If the Fool represents that moment before the Big Bang, then the Magician is the Big Bang itself. He is the number one in the Major Arcana, a number that represents individuality and personal power. We can almost picture him holding that right hand high in the air with a foam finger on it that says, "I'm Number One!" and he'd be justified in doing so. He's making it happen all by himself without help from anyone else.

That right hand pointing up and the left hand pointing down are significant. There is an ancient manuscript called *The Emerald Tablet* that was revered by alchemists and magicians as the sourcebook for creation, or what we now call manifestation. This book begins with this profound phrase: "That which is above is like that which is below." To translate this into common speech, if you can envision it (up in your mind), you can create it (down on Earth). The Magician has the power to create from thought and intention. He represents the force that makes magic happen.

He's working with a set of esoteric tools: the double-pointed wand in his right hand is a conduit for channeling energy both up and down. The belt around his waist is actually an Ouroboros, a snake eating its own tail, the mystical symbol of the cyclical nature of life, death, and rebirth. In front of him are a sword, a wand, a cup, and a pentacle representing the four suits of the tarot and the four alchemical elements of air, fire, water, and earth.

As the number one card, the Magician represents a primary lesson about our lives as spirits having a human experience. Our spirits come down to this earthly plane to learn through creation and over the course of many lifetimes, bit by bit, we begin to understand our own power. One of the spiritual lessons that we learn is that with clear thought and our will we are able to transform reality. The Magician tells us that we can have or be anything if we focus our intention and will on the outcome and trust that it is done. The Magician represents the creator in all of us, whether we are doing intentional magic, creating art, solving problems, or birthing children. We come down to this life experience to create and the Magician represents that facet of our life.

The Keys to the Treasure Chest—
Key Symbols of The Magician

Arms pointing up and down—if we can dream it, we can create it

Double pointed wand—a tool of focus, focusing our thoughts and will

Headband—focused thoughts are powerful and create our reality

Lemniscate—thought connects us to the infinite nature of the Universe

Lilies—spiritual world

Red and white robes—alchemical union of opposing forces that creates a whole

Red rose—material world

Snake belt—immortality, eternity, cyclical nature of life, death, and rebirth

Sword, wand, cup, and pentacle—using all the elements to have mastery over reality

The Wizard's Words of Wisdom—
What The Magician Signifies in a Reading

Power, individuality, and originality

The whole is greater than the sum of its parts

Thought creates reality

You are a powerful creator

You can have, do, or be anything—without limits

Behind the Mysterious Door—Journal Question
to Explore The Magician More Deeply

What am I creating or what would I like to create?

Magic Words—Affirmation for The Magician

"I am a magical manifestor and can have, be, or do anything."

Your Adventure with the High Priestess

The High Priestess

You enter into a temple where a woman dressed in pale blue robes and a headdress sits with a scroll on her lap and a crescent moon at her feet. She is seated between two pillars: one black, marked with the letter *B*, and another white, marked with the letter *J*. Stretched between the pillars behind her is a veil. Looking past it we can just make out a glimpse of an ocean beyond.

The High Priestess represents the feminine divine, the keeper of esoteric knowledge. In older decks, she was called "The Papess," or the female pope, so she encompasses spiritual power in female form or what is sometimes called "Sophia" or wisdom. She may radiate gentleness and grace, but she's no pushover. Behind her is a veil of conscious awareness that separates you from the great spiritual mysteries found in the unconscious and she is the challenger who questions you to see if you are ready and worthy of receiving those mysteries.

The veil behind her is covered with a pattern of pomegranates and date palms. The pomegranates, like the coins on the Ten of Pentacles, are set in the pattern of the Tree of Life from the Kabbalah, and represent that connection from heaven to earth. Symbolically, The High Priestess is telling us that the secrets behind the veil will give us access to divine wisdom of the highest order. The pomegranate has two meanings. In Christian symbolism, it represents the Church, with the countless seeds representing the people coming together in unity. In ancient Greek symbolism, it signifies the goddess Persephone and her cycle of death and rebirth. The palm tree represents the fertility and abundance of the warm seasons when Persephone is above ground.

Behind the veil we get a peek at a vast calm ocean, symbolizing deep and mysterious arcane wisdom.

The High Priestess's crown is an extension of her crown chakra and her connection to her own divine authority. Her crown is the head-dress of the ancient Egyptian goddess Hathor, the goddess of joy, love, and motherhood. This not only gives her the status of royalty but also shows that she is a divine being herself. The crown is a pair of cow horns (Hathor is represented by the cow) with a solar disc between, but can also be seen as the moon in three phases: waxing, full, and waning.

Her blue and white watery robe is reminiscent of another divine mother: the Virgin Mary, and the cross on her chest reflects that connection to Christianity. The equal-armed cross over her heart symbolizes being at a crossroads as well as the intersection of two opposing forces.

She sits between two pillars, one black and one white with the letters *B* and *J* painted on them. These are the pillars at the entrance of Solomon's Temple, Boaz and Jachin. They represent a gateway into spiritual wisdom, while their black and white color combination is a Masonic motif representing the complementary components of nature. The lotus motif on top of the pillars represents the spiritual enlightenment that this gateway offers and is reflective of the influence of Buddhism and Hinduism.

In her lap she holds a scroll with the letters TORA. This is the Sefer Torah, a handwritten copy of the divine teachings that are central to Judaism. She has part of the scroll revealed and part hidden, representing that she will only share some of her wisdom or will, at least, reveal it slowly.

We see the waxing crescent moon at her feet. The moon represents mystery and secrecy. The realm of the moon is the supernatural: intuition, psychic awareness, spirits, the unconscious, fantasies, and dreams. The waxing moon represents increase and the invitation for wisdom to descend on us. The crescent moon is also a symbol of Islam, as well as of Pagan religions and Neo-Paganism.

When we look at the symbols around her, they come from many religious paths. The High Priestess recognizes that there is wisdom in all religions and she has ascended to such a high level of spiritual knowledge that she has discovered the truth that envelops them all. When we go behind the veil, we too can see the truths as she sees them and reach a higher level of enlightenment.

The Keys to the Treasure Chest—
Key Symbols of The High Priestess

Crescent moon—intuition, psychic connection, Islam, Paganism, Neo-Paganism

Date palms—abundance, fertility

Equal-armed cross—being at the crossroads, Christianity

Headdress—divinity, embodiment of the Goddess, ancient Egyptian religion, Paganism

Lotus—enlightenment, Buddhism, Hinduism

Ocean—vast spiritual unknown, intuition, deep emotion

Pale blue robes—intuitive, tranquil, psychic

Pillars—wisdom, Solomon's temple

Pomegranates—community, ancient Greek religion

The High Priestess—spiritually independent

Torah—traditional wisdom, Judaism

Veil—hidden knowledge, mysteries

The Wizard's Words of Wisdom—
What The High Priestess Signifies in a Reading

Accessing the unconscious

All truths as the one truth

Personal revelation

Secrets and mysteries

The power of the Great Goddess

Behind the Mysterious Door—Journal Question
to Explore The High Priestess More Deeply

What truths do I find in spiritual paths other than my own?

Magic Words—Affirmation for The High Priestess

"I am."

Your Adventure with The Empress

The Empress

You see an Empress sitting on a soft pillowy throne at the place where a field meets the wilderness. She is dressed in a loose, flowing white gown decorated with a pomegranate pattern. She wears a crown made up of twelve stars and a laurel wreath, and holds up a golden scepter. Lying next to her throne is a heart-shaped shield with a Venus symbol emblazoned on it.

The Empress is the Love Goddess. And not just of romantic love. She represents all facets of love: romantic, yes, but also friendship, motherly love, and compassion for all living things. She sits on a throne made of soft red cushions representing the nurturing, comfort, ease, sensuality, and luxury that she brings. The heart-shaped shield next to her throne bears the symbol for Venus, the goddess of love and the sign for female. Shields also signify protection from harm. Her heart is safe.

The Empress wears a crown representing the crown chakra and her divine authority as the goddess Aphrodite/Venus. It is also an emblem of achievement. She is the best, highest, most responsible, and most powerful. Her crown's laurel wreath is the symbol of victory and the twelve stars designate her as the mystical woman of Revelations 12:1 who is "wearing a crown of twelve stars on her head." Twelve is the number of the signs in the zodiac, which is a more subtle clue that The Empress is the Universe with a capital *U*.

Her dress is white to signify the higher self and is decorated with pomegranates that are emblematic of the cycle of life, death, and rebirth. However, they are also shaped like the Venus symbol, so they also indicate the connection between sensual passion and fertility. That dress she is wearing is pretty loose, might it be a maternity dress?

The idea of fertility shows up in the scene around her: tall growing grain, a lush, thick forest behind her, a waterfall splashing down. She represents the fertility of Mother Nature as well as human fertility. There is an ease in nature's fruitfulness. If we want to see the abundance of Mother Nature in action, we generally don't have to do anything except get out of the way and let her do her thing. The same energy is present when this card appears. We don't have to do anything except get out of our own way to get our abundant results. Just let nature take its course.

The Empress holds up a golden scepter establishing her power. Her scepter has a globe at the top representing dominion over the worldly plane and is another reminder that the Empress rules over nature—both the wild parts, like the forest, and the tamed parts, like the wheat field. The waterfall spilling into a still pool at her left represents the water of intuition moving through change, the conscious meeting the unconscious.

The Keys to the Treasure Chest—
Key Symbols of The Empress

Empress—authority, motherly energy

Grain—life-giving abundance, conscious creation

Laurel wreath—victory, triumph over all

Pillowy throne—sensual comfort, yielding

Pomegranates—Persephone, cycle of life, death, rebirth

Scepter—worldly prosperity, power

Shield—protecting the heart, the goddess Aphrodite/Venus

Twelve stars—the Universe, mystical woman

White gown—spiritually connected

Wilderness—Mother Nature, untamed

The Wizard's Words of Wisdom—
What The Empress Signifies in a Reading

A love that encompasses romance, passion, friendship, and nurturing

Abundance coming effortlessly

Ease and comfort

Embodying the love goddess

Fertility and giving birth

Behind the Mysterious Door—Journal Question
to Explore The Empress More Deeply

What abundance has come into my life easily?

Magic Words—Affirmation for The Empress

"Love and abundance flow to me effortlessly."

Your Adventure with The Emperor

The Emperor

A white-haired emperor with a long beard sits upright on a massive stone throne decorated with ram heads. He is dressed in armor and wrapped in a red cloak. In one hand he holds an orb, in the other an ankh-shaped scepter.

The Emperor represents supreme leadership. In ancient times, emperors ruled over both kings and their kingdoms. In our modern times, we might think of an emperor as being the CEO, or perhaps the mob boss. He is someone with the maximum authoritative power over groups of people. The Emperor represents the power of construction and destruction. He can make or break you. He represents authority, dominance, direction, shaping, and stability. He also represents worldly wealth and power, self-discipline, law, tradition, organization, hierarchy, and forming advantageous alliances.

Notice that our Emperor is not dressed in luxurious finery, but in protective armor. Armor is not a frivolous clothing choice. It was an outrageously expensive thing to own, but necessary for someone who expects to be in battle. Is he prepared for an attack or is he a warmonger? Is he wearing it hidden under his robe because he's serving in a more peaceful capacity or because he wants to catch his enemies off guard?

His crown legitimizes his authority and his long white beard symbolizes wisdom from experience and age. It also represents having a long life and endurance. For a warrior-emperor like this, to live to an old age would require exceptional skill as well as luck. He has earned his role of leadership. His scepter is an ankh, the Egyptian symbol of eternal life, the symbol of the gods and pharaohs. In his other hand, he holds an orb, symbol of authority and another way of saying, "I rule the world."

His stone throne represents absolute stability but is also unyielding and can indicate that he can be a bit stubborn. Can he possibly be comfortable on that stone throne? Doubtful. But he is willing to sacrifice comfort and be disciplined to gain the necessary security. His throne is decorated with ram heads representing the astrological sign Aries and its attributes: drive, intensity, competitiveness, resilience, action, combativeness, and even headstrong energy. His red robe represents his mastery over the material world. The red robe, rocky orange mountains, and orange sky also reflect the red planet Mars, which is the ruling planet of Aries. That red is the red of life-blood, fire, energy, action, and will. Those mountains are a symbol of climbing to higher places, transcending the typical human experience, and reaching beyond the ordinary. When the Emperor card shows up, you may be given a trial that is meant to test your strength or reveal your weakness. Meet the challenge head on and use the information for improvement.

The river below him represents life still flowing amongst all the harshness of the environment around him. It also represents the never-ending force of change that prevails. No matter how stubbornly the Emperor clings to stability, things will change.

The Keys to the Treasure Chest— Key Symbols of The Emperor

Ankh-shaped scepter—eternal life, Pharaoh

Armor—aggressive, assertive

Crown—divinely given authority

Emperor—ultimate power and authority, the buck stops here

Orb—secular rule

Ram heads—daring, courageous, confident, impatient

Red cloak—worldly authority

Rocky mountains—stubbornness, endurance

Stone throne—rigidity, permanence

White hair and beard—longevity, endurance, grit

The Wizard's Words of Wisdom— What The Emperor Signifies in a Reading

Ambition and competition

Authority over others, self-control

Dealing with institutions

Tradition, leadership, rules

Worldly achievement

Behind the Mysterious Door—Journal Question to Explore The Emperor More Deeply

What do I have the power to control?

Magic Words—Affirmation for The Emperor

"I control my destiny."

Your Adventure with The Hierophant

The Hierophant

You step into a church where a pope is sitting on a throne. He is wearing a triple crown and red robes. In his left hand, he holds a three-armed cross, his right is raised in blessing. Two monks kneel in front of him.

Before we begin exploring the Hierophant, let's jump to the burning question I know you're thinking right now, "What the heck is a hierophant?" Well, don't feel bad for not knowing. Nobody nowadays knows what one is. To find a hierophant you'd have to head back to ancient Greece and find a celebration of the Eleusinian Mysteries. These secret rites celebrated Demeter, goddess of the harvest, and to participate in these mysteries one had to swear a vow of secrecy. The participants seem to have done a great job in keeping that secret. As of today, we have very skimpy information on what exactly went on at the Eleusinian Mysteries, but we do know that it culminated in the showing of sacred objects. The priests leading these rites were called hierophants, a name that comes from the words *hiera*, "holy," and *phainein*, "to show," so in essence, a hierophant is a person who reveals the sacred to us.

The Hierophant in the tarot represents someone who holds great traditional wisdom and passes on that wisdom to initiates. In the RWS Tarot, he is depicted as a pope and indeed in most older version of the tarot, this card is called The Pope. I believe this odd juxtaposition is helpful in understanding this card. We have a Catholic leader bearing the name of an ancient Greek priest. That mash-up is a little like the mixture we see on the High Priestess card. It takes us out of the specific religion and opens it up to all religions—giving us the universal high priest who passes down the traditional teachings of an established religion. So, when we see this card in a reading, does it literally mean a priest, minister, rabbi, guru, or imam? It can mean that, but more often it is looking more broadly at someone who is a mentor to another person who is an initiate. It can be an experienced entrepreneur who helps someone just starting out or a published author assisting a new writer. I like to think of the Hierophant as Mr. Miyagi who teaches the Karate Kid to become a champion. At one time Mr. Miyagi was the beginner and was taught by his mentors—now he has found a worthy protégé and is passing his wisdom on to him.

The Hierophant wears red and white robes representing the fact that he is as concerned with worldly matters as he is with spiritual ones. The triple crown he wears is a direct symbol of the pope and represents the pope's three functions as the supreme pastor, teacher, and priest. We can see the triple role of the mentor as one who leads, teaches, and serves. At the top of this papal tiara, we see three nails, which in Christian iconography represent the nails of the crucifixion. Being at the top of his headdress, they signify Christ-consciousness: having the same enlightenment as the spiritually ascended Jesus. The Hierophant's hand is raised in blessing. If you're doing a multi-card reading, it's always worthwhile to see which card turns up to his left, that is, which card the Hierophant is blessing.

The Hierophant holds a staff that has a triple cross, which is another symbol of the papacy. The crossbeams represent the idea of a step-by-step hierarchy. The bottom beam represents humanity, the middle beam is for the angels and souls, and the top beam, the archangels and heaven. This means taking steps over time to achieve higher levels of consciousness or, in a more secular context, higher levels of skill.

The crossed keys at the Hierophant's feet are a symbol of the keys of St. Peter, follower of Jesus and the first pope. The keys signify that the Hierophant has the "keys to the kingdom" which, in this case, are the keys to higher knowledge of any kind.

At the Hierophant's feet we see two acolytes, or "beginner" priests. These represent the mentor's protégés. They have shaved their heads as a commitment to their path. One wears robes decorated in lilies, representing the path of renouncing worldly desire, the other one wears roses, the path of loving the world.

Like the High Priestess, the scene contains two pillars, which represent initiation. The checkerboard pattern at his feet reflects the Masonic imagery of duality.

The Keys to the Treasure Chest—
Key Symbols of The Hierophant

> Crossed keys—unlocking wisdom, guidance
>
> Hand raised in blessing—power to bless, channeling divine energy
>
> Initiate priests—protégés
>
> Lilies—spiritual renunciation, self-denial
>
> Pope—traditional spiritual wisdom, religion, the guru
>
> Red and white robes—spiritual and mundane issues
>
> Roses—worldly love, love of all
>
> Throne—recognition of authority
>
> Triple crown—spiritually connected, multiple roles, wearing many hats
>
> Triple-armed cross—taking the initiates through the steps

The Wizard's Words of Wisdom—
What The Hierophant Signifies in a Reading

> Conforming culturally
>
> Giving up your individuality to support the group
>
> Having or being a mentor, guru, or teacher
>
> Making moral judgments, issues of right and wrong
>
> Passing down traditional wisdom

Behind the Mysterious Door—Journal Questions
to Explore The Hierophant More Deeply

> Who are my mentors? Who am I mentoring?

Magic Words—Affirmation for The Hierophant

> "I receive wisdom and pass it along to help others."

Your Adventure with The Lovers

The Lovers

You step into the Garden of Eden and see Adam and Eve standing side by side. The sun is shining above and a beautiful angel with hair of leaves and flame blesses the two of them. A tree of flame and a fruit tree with a snake entwined in it flank the nude man and woman, while, in the distance, a mountain rises between them.

When this card appears in a reading, most people immediately jump to the thought that this must be about a romantic relationship, and while it can often be about our love life, if we are willing to look a little deeper at the symbolism, it can be about so much more than that.

The Lovers card represents a union. When true lovers come together, we say that the "two have become one." This card is often associated with the sign Gemini, the twins. If you've ever known a set of twins who were referred to as "the twins" then you understand this "two are one" concept beyond a romantic couple. Yes, we see them as individuals, but they are also this other thing—the two of them together. We can see this in couples who are very closely bonded or business partners who are united in their vision. The partners in this image are on equal footing. There is not one who is more powerful than the other, however, they are not identical. They complement one another.

The Lovers card doesn't have to always represent the union of people. It can represent forces within ourselves. We see that the man is looking at the woman, but the woman is looking up at the angel. The man represents the material world concerns while she connects to the spiritual plane. He connects to the spiritual through her. We can even see this connection as the link to consciousness. The practical man looks to the intuitive woman to reach up to the highest spiritual planes of the angel. Intuition and the wild unconscious form the bridge that gets us to divine realms. Regardless of whether The Lovers is about people or internal forces, this card is about unification. Whether it's having help from a partner or integrating your own masculine and feminine sides, this card says that two are better than one.

Adam and Eve are nude, which means innocence and openness. To open up to the magic of the union, you are being asked to be vulnerable. Their hands are open to each other, indicating that they are willing to both give and receive. The angel above them blesses their union. While the love may be pure, the red wings and flaming hair bring passion and earthly desires to this relationship, while the green leaves in the angel's hair and the green grass below ensure that the partnership will be fruitful.

Behind Eve is the Tree of Knowledge with the snake twined around it. The tree represents material desire and in Judeo-Christian symbolism, the snake represents the temptations of material desire. She has her back to both the tree and the snake and is reaching up to higher awareness. However, if we reach back beyond this interpretation of the snake, we find that other cultures hold the snake in reverence as a symbol of our connection to Mother Earth, the goddess, rebirth, transformation, and healing. Likewise, apples in Celtic, Greek, and Norse lore are magical symbols of eternal life. So, the tree can also be interpreted as the Tree of Life, with its fruit offering life, while the tree behind Adam is the Tree of Passion, and the lesson is to balance groundedness with fiery will. The mountains rising up between the Lovers indicate that there are higher spiritual places yet to be attained, leading closer to the sun of enlightenment.

The Keys to the Treasure Chest—
Key Symbols of The Lovers

Angel—divine blessings, high vibration connection

Flames—passion, will

Fruit tree—knowledge, fruitfulness

Leaves and grass—fertility, life

Mountain—higher spiritual realms

Nudity—openness, innocence

Snake—temptation, rebirth, transformation

Sun—enlightenment, truth

Woman and man—partnership, integration

The Wizard's Words of Wisdom—
What The Lovers Signify in a Reading

Connection to the divine

Finding the path to divine realms

Harmony, balance, and equality

Loving partnerships and commitment

Unifying different forces

Behind the Mysterious Door—Journal Questions
to Explore The Lovers More Deeply

Who are my partners? What can I do to bring more
unification between us?

Magic Words—Affirmation for The Lovers

"I attract the perfect partners to me."

Your Adventure with The Chariot

The Chariot

Outside of a walled city, you meet up with a driver in a chariot. He's dressed in mystical armor and in front of his vehicle sit a black sphinx and a white sphinx.

The Chariot card symbolizes movement and mastery over the material realm. The movement can mean something as practical and pragmatic as moving to a new home or travelling, but just as often it has the essence of progress and moving forward with something. The charioteer is victorious and pushes his life forward. The chariot itself expresses movement into the future. The sphinxes are not hitched up and we do not see any motion yet, but the potential is there. When it shows up in a reading, we are reminded that there may be one last thing that needs to be done to get things moving. Instead of reins, he holds a magic wand. Is this how he controls the sphinxes? That wand is a reminder of the importance of will in controlling our own destiny.

The charioteer is wearing the armor of a mystical warrior. His shoulder epaulets are the faces of crescent moons. These waxing and waning moons represent the *Urim* and *Thummim*—two oracular objects that were part of the breastplate worn by the high priest of the ancient Jewish Temple. He wears armor, a belt, and an apron covered with geomantic and astrological symbols to protect him both physically and spiritually. His laurel wreath crown shows that he is victorious and connects him to the divine. The eight-pointed star on his crown represents his powers of regeneration and his connection to the goddess.

Above the charioteer is a canopy of stars representing the limitlessness of his endeavors. On the front of the chariot, we see the emblem of a winged sun disc representing the Greek god Helios who drives the sun chariot across the sky each day. Below that we see a lingam and yoni, symbolizing the unification of male and female.

The sphinxes symbolize the opposing forces within each of us working in unison. The Greek philosopher Plato referred to our soul as a charioteer trying to drive a black horse and a white horse, the first representing our primal instincts, the other, moral and rational thought. We need the skill to control them both to achieve enlightenment. The good charioteer knows that they won't work together naturally, but is able to keep them under his control through his will.

Behind the chariot, we see a walled city. The charioteer is leaving behind structure and safety and venturing out of his comfort zone. The water behind him is the soul and intuition that he is able to draw from for assistance.

The Keys to the Treasure Chest— Key Symbols of The Chariot

Chariot—movement, relocation, travel

Charioteer—control, mastery, expertise

Laurel wreath crown with stars—victory, connection to the feminine divine

Moon epaulets—magic, divination

Sphinxes—oppositional forces working together, unharnessed energy

Star canopy—limitlessness, the sky's the limit

Symbols on armor—spiritual protection

Wand—magician, control

Winged sun—god-like power

Yoni and lingam—union, masculine and feminine energies

The Wizard's Words of Wisdom—
What The Chariot Signifies in a Reading

Drive leading to success

Movement, travel, or moving house

Obstacles being removed and the road opening

Self-control and control over internal forces

Will, control, and mastery over the situation

Behind the Mysterious Door—Journal Question
to Explore The Chariot More Deeply

What self-control will lead to faster movement?

Magic Words—Affirmation for The Chariot

"I choose where I go."

Your Adventure with Strength

Strength

In a meadow, you see a lovely lady dressed in a white gown wearing a flower crown and sash. In front of her is a ferocious lion. She's bending down and gently and lovingly closing the lion's mouth. A mystical infinity symbol hovers above her head.

The symbolism on the Strength card often surprises those who are learning about the Tarot. Instead of a big, muscled man, we see a beautiful lady wearing flowers. However, this woman is calmly and bravely closing a lion's mouth. A lion! Now that is strength!

Have you ever seen a talented dog trainer take a rebellious dog and shape it into an obedient one? They do it with love and authority and that is how the woman of the Strength card conveys her power. She is confident and courageous and with that magical combination, she doesn't need to resort to brutality or domination. She is controlling the lion, but with love, care, and kindness. She's the alpha of this relationship. This can mean having the inner resources to control relationships with others or to control the more "animalistic" impulses within. The lion can represent our ego and the egocentric desires we have. When we approach these primal urges with courage and kindness, the lion is subdued. The mountain behind her stands for the challenge that the path of Strength presents. We are always on a journey of control over our natural egocentric impulses.

Her white gown is a symbol of being spiritually attuned and her flower crown is the beauty of her mental state, the opening up and flowering of the mind. The lemniscate, or infinity sign, above her head is a magical symbol of connection to the eternal, that matter is neither created nor destroyed, and that we are eternally reborn. While there are so many spiritual aspects to this card, there are material world aspects that it addresses, as well. The Strength card is often the card of the entrepreneur. She is in charge, and she is willing to persevere until she gets the success that she is aiming for.

The Keys to the Treasure Chest— Key Symbols of Strength

Flowers—blossoming, showing love

Lemniscate—connection to the infinite, eternal life

Lion—primal desire, ego, enemies

Mountain—challenges overcome

White gown—spiritually attuned and aware

Woman—gentleness, kindness

The Wizard's Words of Wisdom— What Strength Signifies in a Reading

Inner strength and control of self or others

Taming the wild beast within or outside of you

Self-empowerment and assertiveness

Perseverance to do it yourself

Confidence and belief in self

Behind the Mysterious Door—Journal Question to Explore Strength More Deeply

What forces do I need to tame?

Magic Words—Affirmation for Strength

"I am empowered."

Your Adventure with The Hermit

The Hermit

At the very top of a snowy mountain peak, you see a hermit dressed in gray robes standing alone, holding up a lamp, and looking down below.

The Hermit is the spiritual seeker, but unlike a typical hermit who just holes up in a cave, this Hermit goes within and then brings the light of his knowledge out to share with others. His white beard is the symbol of someone who has gained wisdom through experience. His gray cloak represents discretion, the choice of focusing on the non-material aspects of life, and the ability to blend in. He supports himself with a staff that symbolizes his passion for spiritual knowledge. In his right hand, he holds out the lamp of enlightenment, not just for himself, but for the world. The six-pointed star shining within the lamp represents the magical merging of the two triangles representing fire and water, will and spirit. He stands at the top of a snowy mountain. He has overcome the obstacles and attained the state of awakened enlightenment and wants to share his discoveries with the world below.

When the Hermit shows up in a reading it's a sign for us to research, gain knowledge, and then share that knowledge with others. It may be spiritual knowledge but can also signify learning more about a mundane topic or even a social situation. It is the card of the teacher, someone who shows others the path. It may be that you are called to instruct others or that "when the student is ready, the teacher will appear." While it may be a person who acts as your teacher, it may be a book, an experience, or a flash of revelation that teaches you.

Sometimes the Hermit can show up when we are isolating, for good or ill. Do we need to take some time to ourselves or do we need to resist our antisocial urges? It's a time to reflect on which will bring us the outcome we are aiming for.

The Keys to the Treasure Chest— Key Symbols of The Hermit

Gray cloak—lack of material attachment, looking within

Hermit—doing it on your own, research

Lamp—sharing your wisdom with the world

Mountain peak—the highest spiritual attainment

Six-pointed star—magic, merging will and spirit

Snow—quiet isolation to receive inner guidance

Staff—self-support, self-reliance

White beard—wisdom, patience

The Wizard's Words of Wisdom— What The Hermit Signifies in a Reading

Inner knowing, listening to the voice within

Reflection and looking within

Research and self-study

Solitude, doing it on your own

Solo projects and self-reliance

Behind the Mysterious Door—Journal Question to Explore The Hermit More Deeply

What can I gain by bringing more solitude into my life?

Magic Words—Affirmation for The Hermit

"My inner guidance leads me to enlightenment and wisdom."

Your Adventure with the Wheel of Fortune

Wheel of Fortune

A magical wheel inscribed with mystic symbols floats in a cloudy sky. Three creatures are rotating on the wheel, a snake, a jackal-headed man, and a sphinx. On the clouds around the wheel sit four more winged figures holding books: an angel, a lion, an ox, and an eagle.

Before Las Vegas, before roulette, way back in the medieval era, there was the *Rota Fortuna* or the wheel of fortune. The wheel of fortune was a philosophical concept that expressed the ups and downs of life, not just the risks of gambling, but that life itself was a game whose outcome was beyond the control of the people playing. Today, most of us hold the belief that if we work hard and persevere, we will win, but medieval folks believed that a person's fate wasn't in his control. They believed that you just had to make the best of the hand that was dealt to you. The wheel also reflects the idea of cycles in nature and life and when this card shows up in a reading it is useful to look objectively at the cycles that may be repeating and whether they are helpful or holding us back.

There are numerous symbolic references in this card to the biblical Ezekiel's wheel. In the Book of Ezekiel, the prophet describes his vision of a visitation by Yahweh. In this vision, angelic creatures with four faces: human, lion, ox, and eagle, appear next to a "wheel within a wheel." We can see the representation of these angelic creatures in the four corners around this card's wheel. The strange symbols on the outer wheel are the letters that spell out TARO, TORA, and ROTA, signifying tarot, Torah, and the Latin word for "wheel" respectively. Between those letters, are the Hebrew letters for the magical name of the Jewish god, Yahweh: *Yod Heh Vav Heh.* On the inner wheel are the eight spokes of infinite cycling and the symbols for mercury, sulfur, water, and salt—the alchemical versions of air, fire, water, and earth.

The three figures on the wheel represent the ways that fate can move our lives. The sphinx at the top of the wheel is the guardian of secrets and also echoes the movement of the Chariot card. The snake can represent rebirth or mean danger. He represents the Greek monster Typhon. The jackal-headed man is Anubis, the Egyptian god of the afterlife. Even if bad luck befalls us, we will rise again. The clouds surrounding the wheel represent things that have yet to be, as well the concept that going around the wheel helps raise us to a higher spiritual place.

The Keys to the Treasure Chest—
Key Symbols of the Wheel of Fortune

Angel, lion, ox, and eagle—angelic beings

Clouds—mystery, mysticism

Jackal-headed man—Anubis, afterlife

Mercury, sulfur, water, and salt—the four elements

Snake—rebirth, danger

Sphynx—occult secrets

TARO/TORA/ROTA—tarot, Torah, wheel

Wheel—change, movement, cycle of birth, death, and rebirth

Yod-Heh-Vav-Heh—magical empowered name of Yahweh

The Wizard's Words of Wisdom—
What the Wheel of Fortune Signifies in a Reading

Altering your fate

Changing your luck

Repeating a cycle

Risks leading to rewards

Transformation

Behind the Mysterious Door—Journal Question to Explore the Wheel of Fortune More Deeply

What do I want to change in my life?

Magic Words—Affirmation for the Wheel of Fortune

"Every day I am evolving."

Your Adventure with Justice

Justice

You step into a room and see a woman sitting on a stone bench between two columns. In one hand she holds up a sword, in the other she holds a balance. A veil is stretched between the columns, obscuring what is on the other side.

The Justice card is about karmic justice. If the Wheel of Fortune is about the randomness of life, the Justice card represents the opposite idea—that everything will balance out in the end, that there is order within the chaos of life, and that we will "reap what we sow." The Justice card is like a cosmic slot machine. If we continue to put positive effort toward a certain outcome, Justice reminds us that eventually we will hit the jackpot. Mundane examples of this can be seen in things like looking for a job. We knock on multiple doors and then eventually the perfect one opens. Each time we submit a resume or ask a friend if they know of any job openings, we are dropping another coin in the slot and building up the jackpot that is being held in escrow. These actions weigh down one of the sides of the scale that Justice is holding so that the Universe must bring us what we are aiming for to balance it. Justice is about all "laws" and the law of attraction is a law, just as the law of gravity is a law. What we put out there comes back to us.

The crown that Justice is wearing represents authority that is divinely ordained. Her red gown represents connection to manifestation in the material world. The square shapes on her crown and the clasp on her robe symbolize the structure of laws and rules. Her sword emphasizes the importance of clarity of thought and how thoughts create our reality. The pillars here represent the portal of transformation.

We have the opportunity to change our fate, even if the cloth between those portals hides what the outcome will be. Justice is not wearing a blindfold. She is clear sighted and can envision our future reality.

The Keys to the Treasure Chest— Key Symbols of Justice

Columns—gateway, initiation

Crown—divine insight, wisdom

Green cloak—growth, evolution

Justice—laws, structure, law of attraction

Red gown—material manifestation

Scales—what you put out will come back, everything balances out

Squares—structure, rules, governing

Stone bench—stability, groundedness

Sword—clarity, precision

Veil—unknown outcomes

The Wizard's Words of Wisdom— What Justice Signifies in a Reading

Activating the law of attraction

Finding balance

Investing in the long term

Resolving legal issues fairly

Understanding that what you put into it, you get out of it

Behind the Mysterious Door—Journal Question to Explore Justice More Deeply

What do I need to invest in over the long haul?

Magic Words—Affirmation for Justice

"My thoughts, words, and actions activate my good outcomes."

Your Adventure with The Hanged Man

The Hanged Man

A man is hanging upside down by his foot on a T-shaped gallows tree. Rather than dying or suffering, he stares ahead serenely. Around his head shines a golden aura.

When the Hanged Man shows up in a reading, most people say, "Yikes!"—but look more closely. We see here a man being hung by his foot, not by the neck. He is alive and the expression on his face is peaceful. In fact, with that halo around his head, he is radiating enlightenment. So what's the deal with this guy? Is he an extreme yogi or something?

This image actually comes from Norse mythology—the god Odin, the Allfather, saw the *Norns*, the Norse fate goddesses, inscribing mysterious symbols on *Yggdrasil*, the World Tree. These symbols were *runes* and were not just an alphabet of letters that could spell out words. Each letter held powers that could effect magical change out in the world and only the Norns understood them. In essence, the Norns controlled the world through their control of the runes and Odin wanted some of that sweet magic! To master the runes, Odin hung himself by the foot on the World Tree, pierced his own side with a spear and hovered between life and death for nine days. At the end of the nine days, he received the enlightenment of understanding the runes and being able to access their magical power.

When we see the Hanged Man in a reading, it can indicate that a sacrifice (in the discipline sense, not in the loss sense) is necessary to get what you seek. It can also point to things being in suspension in some way. Things are not moving now, but there is enlightenment that will be gained in this stillness and immobility.

There is also a quality of a shamanic initiation about the subject at hand. With some intense sacrifice, an amazing burst of understanding will be revealed to you. Shamans are initiated through a rite of passage. Don't shrink away from something that feels like a trial or a test—it is the path to your greatness.

The Keys to the Treasure Chest—
Key Symbols of The Hanged Man

Blue tunic—entering psychic dream realms

Halo—enlightenment, awakening the crown chakra

Hanging man—turned upside down, being in suspension, sacrifice, discipline, and diligence

Red leggings—awareness of the material world

Tree—connection to other realms, walking the path between the spirit world and material world

The Wizard's Words of Wisdom—
What The Hanged Man Signifies in a Reading

Discipline and diligence leading to enlightenment

Shamanic initiation

Surrendering to the situation

Temporarily in suspension

Things getting turned upside down

Behind the Mysterious Door—Journal Question
to Explore the Hanged Man More Deeply

Where can I bring more discipline into my life?

Magic Words—Affirmation for the Hanged Man

"I surrender to open up to my enlightenment."

Your Adventure with Death

Death

A skeletal figure in black armor rides a white horse and carries a black flag bearing the emblem of a white rose. He has knocked down one person and is about to fell three more. The sun appears between two towers in the distance.

When the Death card comes up in a reading, people are often shocked and dismayed or at the very least taken aback. I blame Hollywood for this. How many times have we seen a fortune-teller in a movie turn over the Death card and pronounce that someone was about to die? Even without this negative publicity, the Death card gets a bad rap just because its name "death" doesn't usually hold a positive connotation for most people. In modern tarot decks, I've seen the Death card renamed Transformation, The Close, and Transition and these names more closely reflect what this card is about: the change from one thing to another.

There are two Major Arcana cards that cover change, one is The Tower (which you will be discovering in a few pages) and the other is Death. Why two? The Tower has a sense of sudden change that comes from an external place. Death, on the other hand, reflects a change that is born from within. This card is about pruning away the things that no longer serve us. If we have a fruit tree and some of the branches are not bearing fruit, it's useful to cut those particular branches back so that the food that the roots pull up is all channeled to the branches that are producing. When the Death card comes up, the question to ask oneself is "What do I need to prune?" Change affects everyone. There is no life without change. So, rather than refer to the figure as Death, let's refer to him as Change.

Change is a noble knight. He's serving a higher purpose and comes with compassion. He isn't carrying a scythe like the Grim Reaper, he's carrying a flag with the mystic rose symbolizing life and rebirth. Matter can neither be created nor destroyed, it just transforms. So whatever is changing is not disappearing but transforming into something new. The black field of the flag indicates that there are "no rules" when it comes to change. Anything goes. Change is riding a white horse, a symbol of magic and transcendence. The gray sky above him reflects his neutrality. Change is neither bad nor good—it's just change.

Many of the archetypes from other cards are revisited in this one. At the feet of the horse, we see the Hierophant, the Emperor, the child who appears on the Sun card, and the maiden of the Strength card. Each of these reflects a different approach to change. The Emperor resists change and is overcome anyway. The child of the Sun embraces change with no fear. The Hierophant tries to bargain his way out of change, while the Strength card's maiden gracefully surrenders. We also see the towers of the Moon card in the distance, indicating the gateway of transformation that leads to the dawning of a new day. Like the little ship sailing on the river of movement and change, we can flow gracefully toward that new day and the transformation, transcendence, and growth that this card brings.

The Keys to the Treasure Chest—
Key Symbols of Death

Black flag—no rules, no allegiance

Boat—flowing easily toward change

Child—embracing change

Emperor—resistance

Hierophant—bargaining

Maiden—surrender

Skeletal figure—primary essence, getting down to the "bare bones"

Sun—a new day dawns

Towers—transformation, initiation

White horse—spirit realm, transcendence

White rose—spiritually blossoming, rebirth

The Wizard's Words of Wisdom—
What Death Signifies in a Reading

An old phase ends and a new one begins

Flowing with your metamorphosis

Gentle change and mutation

Profound transformation initiated by the self

Pruning away what no longer serves you

Behind the Mysterious Door—Journal Question
to Explore Death More Deeply

What do I need to prune from my life?

Magic Words—Affirmation for Death

"I let go to make space for something better."

Your Adventure with Temperance

Temperance

A divine being stands beside a small pond with one foot in the water and one foot on the land. Her red wings are spread as she pours water from one golden goblet into another. A pathway leads from the pond toward a distant mountain pass where a giant crown hovers in the sky.

Temperance is another one of those cards where the word and the image have an enticing gap. The word temperance can mean moderation but to temper something means to make it harder, stronger, and more durable. In the image we see an angelic being pouring water from one golden goblet into another like an alchemist. In some decks, this is called the Art card and it does show up when we need to approach something as an artist would. What makes art "Art"? I mean, what's the difference between a pretty picture and Art? How do we turn lead into gold?

The divine being of the Temperance card has a unique recipe for creating Art and we get some hint as to what that is by certain subtle clues in the image. She stands with one foot on the land and one foot in the water. The foot on the land indicates working within the material world, while the one in the water means diving into the spiritual. By blending the spiritual and the material, we create something moving, something that touches the soul. We create gold. The path on the left side of the card leads to a golden crown in the sky. If we integrate the spiritual and the material in our journey, our success is assured.

The irises at the pool's edge indicate that this is not actually an angel, but the goddess Iris, the messenger of the Greek gods. The circle on her forehead is a sign of the sun representing all the optimistic visibility of that symbol. Her red wings and white robe are a blending of worldly desire and spiritual elevation. The triangle within a square on her chest has seven sides and represents the seven virtues and the number signifying the high vibration of this card's intention. Since she is a divine messenger, this card may be alerting you to keep your eyes open for divine messages. They are powerful but take an open awareness to see, like the Hebrew Yod-Heh-Vav-Heh hidden at the neckline of her gown.

When we see the Temperance card in a reading, it asks us to adjust our recipe. If we are asking about a material world issue, we may need to add a cup of spirituality to the mix. If we are totally focused on spiritual matters, it may be time to stir in some real-world morsels to see the magic of Spirit made manifest.

The Temperance card often appears when we have access to connections between the spiritual and material worlds. Those connections can be episodes of déjà vu, synchronicities, and, of course, manifesting our wishes. They can also show up as past life connections with others. Those magical moments when we meet someone and we drop into a deep level of connection instantaneously. Have you ever met a new person and fifteen minutes into your conversation, you both tell each other, "I feel like we've been friends for fifteen years"? That's the feeling you have when you meet someone in your soul group with whom you've shared a past life. Cherish those reconnections and what they bring into your life.

The Keys to the Treasure Chest— Key Symbols of Temperance

Crown—success, reaching the highest realms of spirit

Divine being—the goddess Iris, messenger of the gods, divine messages

Golden goblets—vessels of spirit, moving spirit

Mountain pass—bypassing challenges

One foot in the water, one foot on the land—simultaneously in the material and spiritual realms

Pathway—on your spiritual journey

Pond—spiritual depths, still waters run deep

Pouring water—creation, mixing, tempering, healing

Red wings—passion elevates

Sun circlet—positivity, connection to the sun, optimism

Triangle in square emblem—seven blessings

White gown—divinity

Yod-Heh-Vav-Heh—secret divine messages

The Wizard's Words of Wisdom— What Temperance Signifies in a Reading

Awakening to divine messages

Blending the spiritual and the material

Connecting to others through past lifetimes

Finding middle ground and creating balance in our lives

Healing the body or the heart

Behind the Mysterious Door—Journal Question to Explore Temperance More Deeply

How can I elevate material world issues or ground spiritual issues?

Magic Words—Affirmation for Temperance

"Divine messages are everywhere."

Your Adventure with The Devil

The Devil

A horned abomination, half human and half beast, sits atop a stone block. He is holding a torch pointing downward in his left hand, while his right is raised. Chained to the block are a nude man and woman who also have horns.

Here's another card that freaks people out when it shows up in a reading. Nobody wants the Devil showing up, right? It's like you're having this great party and then, dun-dun-DUN, here come the jerk who's going to ruin everything. The Devil card isn't an easy-breezy card, that's for sure, but it's an instructive one and when we confront the Devil in the details, we grow and get past the things that are keeping us chained.

The Devil represents imbalances of power either between people or internally. The Devil figure sits on a stone column to which a man and a woman are chained. In relationships the card can indicate that one person is dominating the other. This can go beyond romantic relationships. Have you ever known someone who had a terrible boss, a dominating parent, or a spoiled child who ran the show? It doesn't have to be just one person either. Sometimes the oppression can alternate between the two people with a game of one-upmanship going back and forth between them like a tennis ball at a match.

The internal power struggles can show up as appetites and addictions. For example, when does taking drugs, drinking, eating, or sex change from recreational fun to an addiction? Are you indulging your animal appetites? If so, are you the master of your appetites or have your appetites enslaved you?

Power struggles can also crop up as defiance. There is a rebellious streak to the Devil card. After all, in Christian lore, the Devil was God's favorite angel who revolted against God's domination and was cast into a lake of fire. Rebellion isn't intrinsically positive or negative. Rebelling in sheer defiance might be a negative, but if you're rebelling against injustice, it would probably be construed as a positive.

So, when the Devil appears we ask ourselves, what's the fight? Are we having a pointless power struggle with someone? Are we having a power struggle with drugs, alcohol, or some other addictive habit? Are we rebelling because of injustice or are we just acting out?

The inverted pentagram above the Devil's head is a symbol of the five elements being turned upside down and chaos reigning. The upside down torch is the fire of passion being turned into addiction. The chained man and woman are a reversed version of Adam and Eve. If you take a closer look at the chains they are wearing, you'll see that they are loosely draped around their necks. They can lift the chains of the struggle up over their heads anytime they wish to be released. The tails of fire and of grapes indicate how materialistic desire can sometimes make us captives. The horns on their heads are a symbol of their indiscriminate promiscuity and show how the illusion of freedom can enslave us.

The Keys to the Treasure Chest—
Key Symbols of The Devil

Chains—oppression, ability to free yourself

Claws—tyranny, others controlling you

Devil—beastly nature, domination

Grapes and flame—slavery to material desire

Hand raised with Jupiter symbol—dominance, dictatorship

Inverted pentagram—chaos, subversion

Inverted torch—passion becoming addiction

The Wizard's Words of Wisdom—
What The Devil Signifies in a Reading

Addictions and impulse control issues

Allowing your own imprisonment

Obsessions and jealous emotions

Power struggles between people or internal struggle

Rebellion against authority

Behind the Mysterious Door—Journal Question
to Explore The Devil More Deeply

What power struggle do I need to free myself from?

Magic Words—Affirmation for The Devil

"I have the power to liberate myself."

Your Adventure with The Tower

The Tower

Against the backdrop of a black sky, a lightning bolt strikes the top of a tall tower built on the summit of a craggy mountain. It knocks off a giant gold crown with a burst of flame. A man and a woman fall from the tower down into the chasm below.

The Tower card is the card of sudden changes coming from external sources. This is necessary change—the Universe clearing out what needs to go. This spiritual "spring cleaning" can be easy or challenging depending on your need to control. It's like the Universe is taking you on a limousine ride to your good outcome. You have a choice to either sit in the back and trust the limo driver to take you to an amazing destination or jump into the front seat and try to take the steering wheel out of the driver's hands. If you let go and ride out the changes, you'll allow the good things to come to you. If you try to control or stop the change, you'll end up driving off the road.

It's that control that is at issue with the Tower. The tower in the image is getting struck by lightning and the old structures are being knocked down to make room for something new. The Tower represents our attachment to the illusion our ego loves to create. Divine intervention will take that down in a flash and give us a chance to learn something in the process. Like a phoenix, we will rise up out of the ashes and into an evolved version of ourselves. There is a hint of this in the symbols. Everything is falling down but it is surrounded by twenty-two yods, or divine blessings. The Universe is blessing us by clearing out this old worthless garbage.

The Keys to the Treasure Chest—
Key Symbols of The Tower

Clouds—unknown outcomes

Crown—authority, ego, worldly achievement

Falling people—surrender, allowing the Universe to remove blocks

Fire—trial by fire, rebirth from the ashes

Lightning—sudden change generated by the Universe

Tower—old structures and systems that need an overhaul

The Wizard's Words of Wisdom—
What The Tower Signifies in a Reading

Blowing your mind wide open

Clearing out what needs to go

Dramatic change creating a clean slate

Making space for a new beginning

Receiving a wake-up call

Behind the Mysterious Door—Journal Question
to Explore The Tower More Deeply

What's another way to view this change?

Magic Words—Affirmation for The Tower

"Everything works out for me so this will work out, too."

Your Adventure with The Star

The Star

You arrive at a quiet grassy plain with small rolling hills under a night sky twinkling with bright stars. In front of you, you see a lovely nude maiden at the edge of a pool of still blue water. She is kneeling at the edge of the water gazing into the tiny pond. She has two water jugs, one in each hand, and is pouring water from them as seven small eight-pointed stars and one enormous star shimmer in the sky above her.

The Star card shows one of the most tranquil scenes in the tarot; what could be more peaceful than a beautiful woman pouring water into a serene reflecting pool under a clear night sky? It's when we look at this image more closely that we start to notice some curious things. First off, the woman is kneeling on one knee with the other foot in the shallows of the pool. She is pouring water from the jugs, but from one she is pouring onto the land, and from the other, she is pouring into the pool.

From a spiritual perspective, the Star card represents a few important principles. It represents the idea of reflection, introspection, and meditation. The beautiful woman is looking at her own reflection in the pool. But we can see that she is not just sitting with her legs crossed and her eyes closed. She has one foot on the land and one foot in the water. Just like Iris in the Temperance card, she is straddling the material/physical world and the spiritual world. We can see the giant star above her pouring its light over her as well. She is receiving the guidance of Spirit above her—she is connected to divine energy through her meditation. She is actively pouring water. On a symbolic level, pouring water means pouring down emotion and spirit. She is taking the love and the light that she has received from the star above her and is pouring that back into the material world (the jug emptying onto the earth) and into the spiritual world (the jug emptying into the water). I think this is one of the most genius aspects of this card—that the woman is not only feeding the world (some say those little plants growing up around her are the hope that she is nurturing and building up with that water)—but that she is also pouring it back into the pool. The pool is where she got the water, so in essence, she is symbolically pouring that spirit back into herself.

When we see the Star card in a reading, immediately the message is about connection with the divine. That connection can show up in so many beautiful ways—being in the flow of creation and making something beautiful, connecting with another soul in divine love, receiving intuitive guidance, spending time in peaceful, natural surroundings—when we think of all the possibilities of how we can connect with divine energy, there are an infinite number. Each of us has our own unique experience of Spirit. How do you know when you are truly connected? You will be completely engrossed and participating in what you are experiencing. Time will become elastic. You will feel as if something or someone is moving through you. There is an otherworldly quality to these moments. We may think they are as rare as lightning striking us, but in reality we can cultivate this flow. Spend time doing the things that connect you to divine energy. Make these activities a priority in your life. If you've never experienced this type of flow, then a great place to start is with meditation—either silent meditation or guided meditation. When you do, you open up to the flow of divine energy, you fill your own cup and as a result have much left over to give others.

The Keys to the Treasure Chest—
Key Symbols of The Star

Bird—taking flight, freedom

Eight-pointed star—connection to the Goddess,
new beginnings

Eight stars—guiding lights

Foot in the pool—one foot in the spiritual world

Foot on the land—one foot in the material world

Mountains—self-care prepares you to reach higher realms

Nudity—innocence, baring it all, vulnerability

Tree—rooted, growth

Water poured into the pool—filling yourself up spiritually

Water poured onto the land—giving to those around you,
nurturing hope, using your spiritual well to take care of
material world concerns

Woman—receptivity, feminine divine

The Wizard's Words of Wisdom—
What The Star Signifies in a Reading

Being a spiritual channel

Focusing on the spiritual aspect of the question at hand

Going beyond the surface and into deep, spiritually connected
relationships

Receiving blessings from heaven

Slowing down, being still, going within, and listening to
your guides

Behind the Mysterious Door—Journal Questions
to Explore The Star More Deeply

Where and when do I feel most connected to divine energy?
How can I bring more of this connection into my life?

Magic Words—Affirmation for The Star

"I am a channel for divine blessings."

Your Adventure with The Moon

The Moon

A pool of water lies in front of you with a path emerging from it, leading over hills, between two towers, and away into the mountains. A crayfish emerges from the water and begins its crawl up the path. To the left of the path, a dog raises his head to howl at the moon. To the right of the path, a wolf does the same. A mysterious moon that is simultaneously full, half, and crescent rains down golden beams of light and floating flames over the scene.

When the Moon shows up, it's often an indicator of undefined energy. You won't find structure, rules, regimentation, or discipline surrounding this card. You have to tap in intuitively to whether this lack of definition is a good thing or a bit of a challenge. For those who thrive in structured environments, the undefined nature of the Moon may feel too vague. But for those who thrive in more open-ended worlds, the vagueness of the Moon is a place of freedom. "Finally, nobody is telling me what to do!" The Moon may keep some of the information you need hidden and demand that you find your own path. Like the little crayfish crawling out from the deep water, our deepest emotions and intuition will guide the way.

However, even within this undefined territory, the crayfish is goal-driven and needs to pay attention to her own path. She must walk between the dog, which represents pleasing others at the cost of one's own truth, and the wolf, which represents selfishly only pleasing oneself with no regard for others. If she can navigate the middle ground between those two, she will be showered with beautiful moonbeam blessings, in the form of those fiery yods, and move gracefully between the gateway of the two towers.

Those towers form the doorway of initiation. The gateway represents moving from one world into another, advancing on what you know—initiation, graduation, moving up. Moving through one of these initiatory gateways can be a profound experience because when we move into a new role, the old role is left behind. When we become a child, babyhood is left behind. When we get married, singledom is left behind. When we get promoted to manager, the role of subordinate is left behind. In our Western culture, we tend to put a focus on the new thing gained, but the Moon card also awakens us to the fact that we are simultaneously letting something go. This adds another layer to the undefined quality of the Moon. The Moon reminds us that even when not all the information is known, all is still well. That some of the excitement and fun of our life journey is not knowing all the answers and playing hide-and-seek along the way.

The Keys to the Treasure Chest — Key Symbols of The Moon

Crayfish—deepest desires

Dog—pleasing other people

Fifteen yods—blessings showering down

Moon—mysterious, intuitive, undefined

Mountains—having the tools to meet the challenges ahead

Path—the life journey

Pool—intuition, a deep spiritual well

Rays—reflected light

Two towers—gateway of initiation, transformation

Wolf—selfishness

The Wizard's Words of Wisdom—
What The Moon Signifies in a Reading

Being initiated into a new state of being

Finding a middle path between always pleasing others and complete selfishness

Receiving blessings for being self-guided

Things being undefined or vague

Trusting deep intuition to guide you

Behind the Mysterious Door—Journal Question
to Explore The Moon More Deeply

What deep desire must I bring to the surface?

Magic Words—Affirmation for The Moon

"I balance pleasing myself and pleasing others."

Your Adventure with The Sun

The Sun

You enter into a walled garden where sunflowers are blooming in profusion. The sun is shining brightly overhead in the clear blue sky. A little child gleefully rides around naked on a white horse. She is wearing a flower crown with a red feather in it and waving a large red banner. Her arms are stretched open wide as she radiates the pure joy of her experience.

The Sun card radiates true carefree happiness. The little child is enjoying the moment to the fullest because all is indeed well. Life is nothing but delight and pleasure. All is shown and known; there are no secrets or hidden agendas. The sun shines down to reveal all. Mental, emotional, spiritual, and physical well-being are assured. Enlightenment comes with innocence and elevated high vibration feeling. The benevolent sun god shines down on everyone equally.

The greatest attainment of Spirit is called spiritual enlightenment—it's a state of understanding your reason for being, feeling self-acceptance, and having a clear connection to divine energy. It's not for nothing that we call this state "enlightenment" and that the sun is the biggest bringer of light there is. The highest attainment of spiritual enlightenment comes from always striving to be in a place of joy, happiness, and carefree play. The greatest spiritual masters are not the serious ponderous souls, but those who are in states of openness and joy. This card represents that enlightened state and all that it can attract.

When this card shows up in a reading, it indicates that all is well—health and happiness are assured. It indicates that all is above board, that sharing your light with others will spread joy. You have become spiritually enlightened to the fact that life is meant to be fun and you have the power to attain that. It can also indicate visibility in the best sense. You or your projects are successful and seen widely and appreciated by others.

The Keys to the Treasure Chest—
Key Symbols of The Sun

Arms open wide—confidence, openness

Child—innocence, open-mindedness, being present in the moment

Flower crown—the crown chakra, connection to the divine, your crowning glory

Garden wall—protection from the outside world or negative forces

Red banner—victory on the material plane, fame and recognition

Red feather—reaching up to connect to divine energy, conscious enlightenment

Sun rays—radiating goodness, illuminating the darkness, the divine reaching down to us

Sun—truth, divinity, enlightenment, lightness, being seen by all

Sunflowers—following the sun and facing the light

White horse—power and wisdom, freedom, magical allies

The Wizard's Words of Wisdom—
What The Sun Signifies in a Reading

Carefree joy, happiness, enthusiasm

Confidence and belief in self

Fame and recognition of you or your projects

Good mental, emotional, spiritual, physical health

Truth brought into the light

Behind the Mysterious Door—Journal Question to Explore The Sun More Deeply

What do I need to bring out into the open?

Magic Words—Affirmation for The Sun

"I am all joy, all light, and all love."

Your Adventure with the Judgment Card

Judgment

You pull open a great iron gate and step into an old-fashioned cemetery with grave vaults above the ground. Above you, the Archangel Gabriel emerges from the cloud and blows a long brass horn. As you hear his bracing wake-up call, you see the tombs around you shift, lids begin to move, and people rise up out of the tombs—children, women, and men in whole beautiful bodies—rubbing their eyes and awakening as if from a deep sleep. As they wake up and realize that they are once again alive and in their material form, they begin rejoicing, looking up to Gabriel in gratitude and amazement. You see around you a scene of great happiness as the people spontaneously throw their arms up to thank the angel who released them from death.

The energy behind the Judgment card is exceptionally powerful. It represents the resurrection of the dead on Judgment Day. In the Jewish, Christian, Muslim, and Zoroastrian belief systems, there is a belief that at the end of the world, there will come a day when all of the dead will be raised up and restored to their bodily form—in essence to become immortal. This belief was particularly cherished in medieval times, when the tarot originated.

When this card pops up in a reading, I do sometimes jokingly refer to it as the zombie apocalypse card. I mean, dead people *are* coming back to life, and that woman on the right with her arms stretched out in front of her really isn't helping to calm my fear of undead brain eaters. But when we consider the true essence of this card, it's not about the dead being brought back to life, it's not even about the concept of judgment, but about rebirth, renewal, expansion, and evolution. If you look at this card as the metaphor that it is, people are born, they live, they die, and then, just when you think the story is over, "Bam!" they come back again to be reborn again as something better than they were before. Which makes me think the ancient mystics who came up with this were onto the whole past life thing, but weren't sure how to conceptualize it completely.

Rather than a scene from a B movie, this card's energy is much more like a butterfly emerging from a cocoon. The caterpillar is going along with his life, then decides it's time to go into the cocoon, does a little metamorphosis thing and, a few weeks later, ta-da! out pops the evolved butterfly, right? Well, sort of. What actually happens in that cocoon is not so pretty. In fact, it's downright disgusting. When the caterpillar gets all snuggled up in its safe little cocoon, it begins to digest itself, essentially turning its body into a soup, which then reconfigures as a butterfly. Gives a whole new meaning to the word "cocooning," doesn't it? Becoming a butterfly is not an easy business—not in the least.

It's the same thing for us when we evolve. We start out with one thing (ourselves, our ideas, our lives) and then a trial of some kind happens and, if we are spiritually open to evolving on our soul's journey and growing, we rebuild and emerge as something more complex, more expanded, and, to be truthful, more beautiful than we were before. There is an element of judgment that comes in at that point of liquefying. When we reach the point of being turned into Cream of Caterpillar soup, we have the opportunity to make a conscious decision, to use our judgment, and decide to take that soup and make it into something. You decide whether to evolve and become a butterfly or devolve into warmed-over caterpillar consommé. So when this card comes up, it may be about being in the midst of that soup-making or it may be about being the butterfly and allowing your wings to stretch and expand before you can fly.

The Keys to the Treasure Chest—
Key Symbols of the Judgment Card

Archangel Gabriel—divine messenger, spiritual blessings

Clouds—heavenly energy, the separation of the realms of heaven and earth

Horn—wake-up call, having a new calling

Mountains—meeting challenges, spiritual elevation

Open coffins—opening up, coming out of the cocoon, emergence

People rising up—waking up to a new consciousness, rebirth, evolution, expansion

White flag with red cross—decisiveness, victory, decision-making

The Wizard's Words of Wisdom—
What the Judgment Card Signifies in a Reading

Awakening to a new and improved version

Evolving on your life path

Expanding beyond your comfort zone

Making choices or judgment calls

Transforming from one state to another

Behind the Mysterious Door—Journal Questions
to Explore the Judgment Card More Deeply

How would I like to evolve? What would I like to evolve into?

Magic Words—Affirmation for Judgment

"Everything I experience helps me to evolve."

Your Adventure with The World

The World

In a blue sky we see a beautiful woman floating weightlessly as if she is dancing in the air. She is nude, except for a blue scarf twining around her, and in each hand she holds a wand. Framing her is a large wreath of laurel leaves tied at the top and bottom with a red ribbon, and surrounding that we see four clouds, each with a disembodied head—one cloud has a blond person; another, an eagle; the third, a horned bull; and finally, the fourth, a lion with a thick mane.

The World is the final card of the Major Arcana. It symbolically represents the rebirth of the new heaven on earth after the Judgment Day. This card is so heavily symbolic that without knowing the "code" of what you're seeing, it's hard to discern what's going on here or what this card signifies. I mean, where is the "world" even shown in the World card?

First, we have the woman in the center of the wreath. She is the Anima Mundi or the "world soul." The world soul is a concept that we find in a multitude of philosophies across the globe going back to Plato in ancient Greece. It's the idea that there is one soul that connects us all, that we are all one. So the World card isn't really about the world at all, but the spiritual stuff that connects everything in the world— the stuff that connects the spiritual and the material. Alchemists, who were really proto-scientists trying to figure out the physical realm using spiritual concepts, loved the concept of the Anima Mundi but as science moved farther and farther away from spirituality, we have lost this concept of the world soul. Ah, it pokes it's head out once in awhile—we see movies like *Star Wars*, which mentions "the Force" or the Disney cartoon Pocahontas, where she sings about being connected to the animals, rocks, and plants around her. This concept is that but so much more.

It is about recognizing that beyond being merely connected, everything *is* one. The World card represents that one-ness, and when you truly understand our place in being at one with everything, you have attained enlightenment. Whoa! When we see the World card show up in a reading, it represents wholeness, completion, and fulfillment of our intentions, in other words, manifestation. She holds a wand in each hand to demonstrate that magnificent ability to create her own reality, double the power of the Magician. Often, when I see this card show up in a reading, it can mean that grand intentions are coming to pass or that the person needs to dream bigger because if they do, they can manifest those big dreams.

Those four onlookers in the clouds, the angel, the eagle, the ox, and the lion, are traditional representations of the four Evangelists of the Gospels (Matthew the angel, John the eagle, Luke the ox, and Mark the lion). But they also represent the four elements (angel—water, eagle—air, ox—earth, and lion—fire) and the four angels from Ezekiel that we saw before in the Wheel of Fortune card. The laurel wreath around her represents the circle of life, completeness, and victory.

If we look at the card as a whole, it represents tapping into the spirit of the Universe, in fact in some decks this card is called the Universe. This is the ultimate goal of all spiritual folks: to tap into that greater wisdom, that enlightenment. So, the World card represents the ability to access all that juicy spiritual stuff. It represents waking up and, ultimately, having it all.

The Keys to the Treasure Chest—
Key Symbols of The World

Angel—spiritual nature, connection to the divine, water

Blue sky—all is clear, happiness

Clouds—spiritual messengers

Eagle—focus, concentrated thought, air

Four heads—four Evangelists, four elements, angels

Laurel wreath—victory, success, coming full circle

Lion—courage, sovereignty, ownership, fire

Nude woman—the Anima Mundi (the world soul), pure essence of spirit, nothing to hide

Ox—service, strength, sacrifice, earth

Red ribbon—connection to the material world, tying up loose ends

Scarf—water, the connection to spirit

Wands—skillfulness, master manifestor, all resources being utilized

The Wizard's Words of Wisdom— What The World Signifies in a Reading

Connecting to the highest realms

Doing something for a higher purpose

Dreaming bigger

Satisfying your aims and desires

Things coming to a fulfilling conclusion

Behind the Mysterious Door—Journal Questions to Explore The World More Deeply

What is my biggest dream? How can I support myself in allowing that dream to become a fire within me?

Magic Words—Affirmation for The World

"I connect to the highest realms of spirit."

[18]

Where Do I Take My Adventure from Here?

You did it! You have had seventy-eight adventures—one with each of the tarot cards. You've traveled to places that only exist in the imagination, you've hung out with Kings, Queens, and Knights, you've done unbelievable things and conquered impossible tasks. Where do you go from here?

If you've been faithfully recording your daily cards in your tarot journal, then you are ready to start reading for others. Start with one card readings for friends and family. Ask them if they have a question or which area of their life they would like to explore. Shuffle the cards, say a blessing, then turn over a single card. Read the card just as if you are analyzing it for your journal. Go over what you see and then start drawing out the symbolism and how it relates to their question. Trust that the message that you are giving them will be helpful to them, either now or in the future.

Once you've mastered one card readings, you can move on to larger, more complex spreads, such as past/present/future three card readings or even a ten card Celtic Cross reading. Look up different layouts online, test them out. and see which ones are the most useful for you. Trust your own guidance and the meaning that you have discovered in your adventures with the tarot.

Most importantly, enjoy spending time with the cards. My biggest wish for you is that you continue a life-long journey with the tarot and receive all the love and light that it has to share with you.

Glossary

affirmation—Positive words of intention written or spoken out loud to obtain a result

Anima Mundi—The world soul, the energy that connects everything

court cards—The Page, Knight, Queen, and King of the deck

elements—The four elements of ancient times—air, fire, water, and earth—corresponding to qualities that these natural phenomena possess

law of attraction—The belief that "like attracts like" and that our thoughts and beliefs will attract the thing that we are focused on

lemniscate—A figure eight on its side, the infinity symbol

lingam and yoni—Hindu symbols of male and female, creation and regeneration

Major Arcana—The twenty-two cards numbered zero through twenty-one representing larger spiritual themes

Minor Arcana—The fifty-six cards numbered one through ten, Page, Knight, Queen, and King, broken up into fours suits

occult—Hidden spiritual knowledge

pips—The "spots" on a Minor Arcana card, for example, the Four of Cups has four pips

RWS—The Rider-Waite-Smith Tarot deck

suits—The division of the Minor Arcana into families—Swords, Wands, Cups, and Pentacles

synchronicity—Meaningful coincidences or unrelated events that line up to send us a message

trumps—The Major Arcana

yods—Symbol for spiritual blessings, the first letter of the ineffable name of the Jewish god

About the Author

Madame Pamita is a tarot scholar, professional reader, and rootworker. She is the owner of Madame Pamita's Parlour of Wonders, an old-time spiritualist's shop in Los Angeles, where she offers tarot readings in her salon, teaches classes in tarot and magic, and creates spiritual/magical tools for transforming lives.

Visit her online at *www.parlourofwonders.com*.

To Our Readers

Weiser Books, an imprint of Red Wheel/Weiser, publishes books across the entire spectrum of occult, esoteric, speculative, and New Age subjects. Our mission is to publish quality books that will make a difference in people's lives without advocating any one particular path or field of study. We value the integrity, originality, and depth of knowledge of our authors.

Our readers are our most important resource, and we appreciate your input, suggestions, and ideas about what you would like to see published.

Visit our website at *www.redwheelweiser.com* to learn about our upcoming books and free downloads, and be sure to go to *www.redwheelweiser.com/newsletter* to sign up for news-letters and exclusive offers.

You can also contact us at *info@rwwbooks.com* or at

Red Wheel/Weiser, LLC
65 Parker Street, Suite 7
Newburyport, MA 01950